C-462   CAREER EXAMINATION SERIES

This is your
PASSBOOK for...

Mail Handler (USPS)

Test Preparation Study Guide
Questions & Answers

COPYRIGHT NOTICE

This book is SOLELY intended for, is sold ONLY to, and its use is RESTRICTED to individual, bona fide applicants or candidates who qualify by virtue of having seriously filed applications for appropriate license, certificate, professional and/or promotional advancement, higher school matriculation, scholarship, or other legitimate requirements of education and/or governmental authorities.

This book is NOT intended for use, class instruction, tutoring, training, duplication, copying, reprinting, excerption, or adaptation, etc., by:

1) Other publishers
2) Proprietors and/or Instructors of "Coaching" and/or Preparatory Courses
3) Personnel and/or Training Divisions of commercial, industrial, and governmental organizations
4) Schools, colleges, or universities and/or their departments and staffs, including teachers and other personnel
5) Testing Agencies or Bureaus
6) Study groups which seek by the purchase of a single volume to copy and/or duplicate and/or adapt this material for use by the group as a whole without having purchased individual volumes for each of the members of the group
7) Et al.

Such persons would be in violation of appropriate Federal and State statutes.

PROVISION OF LICENSING AGREEMENTS – Recognized educational, commercial, industrial, and governmental institutions and organizations, and others legitimately engaged in educational pursuits, including training, testing, and measurement activities, may address request for a licensing agreement to the copyright owners, who will determine whether, and under what conditions, including fees and charges, the materials in this book may be used them. In other words, a licensing facility exists for the legitimate use of the material in this book on other than an individual basis. However, it is asseverated and affirmed here that the material in this book CANNOT be used without the receipt of the express permission of such a licensing agreement from the Publishers. Inquiries re licensing should be addressed to the company, attention rights and permissions department.

All rights reserved, including the right of reproduction in whole or in part, in any form or by any means, electronic or mechanical, including photocopying, recording, or by any information storage and retrieval system, without permission in writing from the Publisher.

Copyright © 2024 by
National Learning Corporation

212 Michael Drive, Syosset, NY 11791
(516) 921-8888 • www.passbooks.com
E-mail: info@passbooks.com

PUBLISHED IN THE UNITED STATES OF AMERICA

PASSBOOK® SERIES

THE *PASSBOOK® SERIES* has been created to prepare applicants and candidates for the ultimate academic battlefield – the examination room.

At some time in our lives, each and every one of us may be required to take an examination – for validation, matriculation, admission, qualification, registration, certification, or licensure.

Based on the assumption that every applicant or candidate has met the basic formal educational standards, has taken the required number of courses, and read the necessary texts, the *PASSBOOK® SERIES* furnishes the one special preparation which may assure passing with confidence, instead of failing with insecurity. Examination questions – together with answers – are furnished as the basic vehicle for study so that the mysteries of the examination and its compounding difficulties may be eliminated or diminished by a sure method.

This book is meant to help you pass your examination provided that you qualify and are serious in your objective.

The entire field is reviewed through the huge store of content information which is succinctly presented through a provocative and challenging approach – the question-and-answer method.

A climate of success is established by furnishing the correct answers at the end of each test.

You soon learn to recognize types of questions, forms of questions, and patterns of questioning. You may even begin to anticipate expected outcomes.

You perceive that many questions are repeated or adapted so that you can gain acute insights, which may enable you to score many sure points.

You learn how to confront new questions, or types of questions, and to attack them confidently and work out the correct answers.

You note objectives and emphases, and recognize pitfalls and dangers, so that you may make positive educational adjustments.

Moreover, you are kept fully informed in relation to new concepts, methods, practices, and directions in the field.

You discover that you are actually taking the examination all the time: you are preparing for the examination by "taking" an examination, not by reading extraneous and/or supererogatory textbooks.

In short, this PASSBOOK®, used directedly, should be an important factor in helping you to pass your test.

MAIL HANDLER (U.S.P.S.)

DUTIES:

Unloads mail from trucks. Separates all mail received from trucks and conveyors for dispatch to other conveying units and separates and delivers mail for delivery to distribution areas. Places empty sacks or pouches on racks, labels them where prearranged or where racks are plainly marked, dumps mail from sacks, cuts ties, faces letter mail, carries mail to distributors for processing, places processed mail into sacks, removes filled sacks and pouches from racks and closes and locks sacks and pouches. Picks up sacks, pouches, and outside pieces, separates outgoing bulk mails for dispatch and loads mail onto trucks. Handles and sacks empty equipment; inspects empty equipment for mail and restrings sacks. Cancels stamps on parcel post, operates cancelling machines, and carries mail from cancelling machine to distribution area. Assists in supply and slip rooms and operates copy machine and related office equipment. In addition, may perform any of the following duties: make occasional simple distribution of parcel post mail that requires no scheme knowledge; operate electric fork lifts; rewrap damaged parcels; weigh incoming sacks; clean and sweep work areas, offices rest rooms, and trucks where work is not performed by a regular cleaner. Operates equipment and machinery assigned to the jurisdiction of the Mail Handler Union. Performs other duties as assigned.

HOW TO TAKE A TEST

I. YOU MUST PASS AN EXAMINATION

A. *WHAT EVERY CANDIDATE SHOULD KNOW*

Examination applicants often ask us for help in preparing for the written test. What can I study in advance? What kinds of questions will be asked? How will the test be given? How will the papers be graded?

As an applicant for a civil service examination, you may be wondering about some of these things. Our purpose here is to suggest effective methods of advance study and to describe civil service examinations.

Your chances for success on this examination can be increased if you know how to prepare. Those "pre-examination jitters" can be reduced if you know what to expect. You can even experience an adventure in good citizenship if you know why civil service exams are given.

B. *WHY ARE CIVIL SERVICE EXAMINATIONS GIVEN?*

Civil service examinations are important to you in two ways. As a citizen, you want public jobs filled by employees who know how to do their work. As a job seeker, you want a fair chance to compete for that job on an equal footing with other candidates. The best-known means of accomplishing this two-fold goal is the competitive examination.

Exams are widely publicized throughout the nation. They may be administered for jobs in federal, state, city, municipal, town or village governments or agencies.

Any citizen may apply, with some limitations, such as the age or residence of applicants. Your experience and education may be reviewed to see whether you meet the requirements for the particular examination. When these requirements exist, they are reasonable and applied consistently to all applicants. Thus, a competitive examination may cause you some uneasiness now, but it is your privilege and safeguard.

C. *HOW ARE CIVIL SERVICE EXAMS DEVELOPED?*

Examinations are carefully written by trained technicians who are specialists in the field known as "psychological measurement," in consultation with recognized authorities in the field of work that the test will cover. These experts recommend the subject matter areas or skills to be tested; only those knowledges or skills important to your success on the job are included. The most reliable books and source materials available are used as references. Together, the experts and technicians judge the difficulty level of the questions.

Test technicians know how to phrase questions so that the problem is clearly stated. Their ethics do not permit "trick" or "catch" questions. Questions may have been tried out on sample groups, or subjected to statistical analysis, to determine their usefulness.

Written tests are often used in combination with performance tests, ratings of training and experience, and oral interviews. All of these measures combine to form the best-known means of finding the right person for the right job.

II. HOW TO PASS THE WRITTEN TEST

A. NATURE OF THE EXAMINATION

To prepare intelligently for civil service examinations, you should know how they differ from school examinations you have taken. In school you were assigned certain definite pages to read or subjects to cover. The examination questions were quite detailed and usually emphasized memory. Civil service exams, on the other hand, try to discover your present ability to perform the duties of a position, plus your potentiality to learn these duties. In other words, a civil service exam attempts to predict how successful you will be. Questions cover such a broad area that they cannot be as minute and detailed as school exam questions.

In the public service similar kinds of work, or positions, are grouped together in one "class." This process is known as *position-classification*. All the positions in a class are paid according to the salary range for that class. One class title covers all of these positions, and they are all tested by the same examination.

B. FOUR BASIC STEPS

1) Study the announcement

How, then, can you know what subjects to study? Our best answer is: "Learn as much as possible about the class of positions for which you've applied." The exam will test the knowledge, skills and abilities needed to do the work.

Your most valuable source of information about the position you want is the official exam announcement. This announcement lists the training and experience qualifications. Check these standards and apply only if you come reasonably close to meeting them.

The brief description of the position in the examination announcement offers some clues to the subjects which will be tested. Think about the job itself. Review the duties in your mind. Can you perform them, or are there some in which you are rusty? Fill in the blank spots in your preparation.

Many jurisdictions preview the written test in the exam announcement by including a section called "Knowledge and Abilities Required," "Scope of the Examination," or some similar heading. Here you will find out specifically what fields will be tested.

2) Review your own background

Once you learn in general what the position is all about, and what you need to know to do the work, ask yourself which subjects you already know fairly well and which need improvement. You may wonder whether to concentrate on improving your strong areas or on building some background in your fields of weakness. When the announcement has specified "some knowledge" or "considerable knowledge," or has used adjectives like "beginning principles of…" or "advanced … methods," you can get a clue as to the number and difficulty of questions to be asked in any given field. More questions, and hence broader coverage, would be included for those subjects which are more important in the work. Now weigh your strengths and weaknesses against the job requirements and prepare accordingly.

3) Determine the level of the position

Another way to tell how intensively you should prepare is to understand the level of the job for which you are applying. Is it the entering level? In other words, is this the position in which beginners in a field of work are hired? Or is it an intermediate or advanced level? Sometimes this is indicated by such words as "Junior" or "Senior" in the class title. Other jurisdictions use Roman numerals to designate the level – Clerk I, Clerk II, for example. The word "Supervisor" sometimes appears in the title. If the level is not indicated by the title, check the description of duties. Will you be working under very close supervision, or will you have responsibility for independent decisions in this work?

4) Choose appropriate study materials

Now that you know the subjects to be examined and the relative amount of each subject to be covered, you can choose suitable study materials. For beginning level jobs, or even advanced ones, if you have a pronounced weakness in some aspect of your training, read a modern, standard textbook in that field. Be sure it is up to date and has general coverage. Such books are normally available at your library, and the librarian will be glad to help you locate one. For entry-level positions, questions of appropriate difficulty are chosen – neither highly advanced questions, nor those too simple. Such questions require careful thought but not advanced training.

If the position for which you are applying is technical or advanced, you will read more advanced, specialized material. If you are already familiar with the basic principles of your field, elementary textbooks would waste your time. Concentrate on advanced textbooks and technical periodicals. Think through the concepts and review difficult problems in your field.

These are all general sources. You can get more ideas on your own initiative, following these leads. For example, training manuals and publications of the government agency which employs workers in your field can be useful, particularly for technical and professional positions. A letter or visit to the government department involved may result in more specific study suggestions, and certainly will provide you with a more definite idea of the exact nature of the position you are seeking.

III. KINDS OF TESTS

Tests are used for purposes other than measuring knowledge and ability to perform specified duties. For some positions, it is equally important to test ability to make adjustments to new situations or to profit from training. In others, basic mental abilities not dependent on information are essential. Questions which test these things may not appear as pertinent to the duties of the position as those which test for knowledge and information. Yet they are often highly important parts of a fair examination. For very general questions, it is almost impossible to help you direct your study efforts. What we can do is to point out some of the more common of these general abilities needed in public service positions and describe some typical questions.

1) General information

Broad, general information has been found useful for predicting job success in some kinds of work. This is tested in a variety of ways, from vocabulary lists to questions about current events. Basic background in some field of work, such as sociology or economics, may be sampled in a group of questions. Often these are principles which have become familiar to most persons through exposure rather than through formal training. It is difficult to advise you how to study for these questions; being alert to the world around you is our best suggestion.

2) Verbal ability

An example of an ability needed in many positions is verbal or language ability. Verbal ability is, in brief, the ability to use and understand words. Vocabulary and grammar tests are typical measures of this ability. Reading comprehension or paragraph interpretation questions are common in many kinds of civil service tests. You are given a paragraph of written material and asked to find its central meaning.

3) Numerical ability

Number skills can be tested by the familiar arithmetic problem, by checking paired lists of numbers to see which are alike and which are different, or by interpreting charts and graphs. In the latter test, a graph may be printed in the test booklet which you are asked to use as the basis for answering questions.

4) Observation

A popular test for law-enforcement positions is the observation test. A picture is shown to you for several minutes, then taken away. Questions about the picture test your ability to observe both details and larger elements.

5) Following directions

In many positions in the public service, the employee must be able to carry out written instructions dependably and accurately. You may be given a chart with several columns, each column listing a variety of information. The questions require you to carry out directions involving the information given in the chart.

6) Skills and aptitudes

Performance tests effectively measure some manual skills and aptitudes. When the skill is one in which you are trained, such as typing or shorthand, you can practice. These tests are often very much like those given in business school or high school courses. For many of the other skills and aptitudes, however, no short-time preparation can be made. Skills and abilities natural to you or that you have developed throughout your lifetime are being tested.

Many of the general questions just described provide all the data needed to answer the questions and ask you to use your reasoning ability to find the answers. Your best preparation for these tests, as well as for tests of facts and ideas, is to be at your physical and mental best. You, no doubt, have your own methods of getting into an exam-taking mood and keeping "in shape." The next section lists some ideas on this subject.

IV. KINDS OF QUESTIONS

Only rarely is the "essay" question, which you answer in narrative form, used in civil service tests. Civil service tests are usually of the short-answer type. Full instructions for answering these questions will be given to you at the examination. But in case this is your first experience with short-answer questions and separate answer sheets, here is what you need to know:

1) Multiple-choice Questions

Most popular of the short-answer questions is the "multiple choice" or "best answer" question. It can be used, for example, to test for factual knowledge, ability to solve problems or judgment in meeting situations found at work.

A multiple-choice question is normally one of three types—
- It can begin with an incomplete statement followed by several possible endings. You are to find the one ending which *best* completes the statement, although some of the others may not be entirely wrong.
- It can also be a complete statement in the form of a question which is answered by choosing one of the statements listed.

- It can be in the form of a problem – again you select the best answer.

Here is an example of a multiple-choice question with a discussion which should give you some clues as to the method for choosing the right answer:

When an employee has a complaint about his assignment, the action which will *best* help him overcome his difficulty is to
- A. discuss his difficulty with his coworkers
- B. take the problem to the head of the organization
- C. take the problem to the person who gave him the assignment
- D. say nothing to anyone about his complaint

In answering this question, you should study each of the choices to find which is best. Consider choice "A" – Certainly an employee may discuss his complaint with fellow employees, but no change or improvement can result, and the complaint remains unresolved. Choice "B" is a poor choice since the head of the organization probably does not know what assignment you have been given, and taking your problem to him is known as "going over the head" of the supervisor. The supervisor, or person who made the assignment, is the person who can clarify it or correct any injustice. Choice "C" is, therefore, correct. To say nothing, as in choice "D," is unwise. Supervisors have and interest in knowing the problems employees are facing, and the employee is seeking a solution to his problem.

2) True/False Questions

The "true/false" or "right/wrong" form of question is sometimes used. Here a complete statement is given. Your job is to decide whether the statement is right or wrong.

SAMPLE: A roaming cell-phone call to a nearby city costs less than a non-roaming call to a distant city.

This statement is wrong, or false, since roaming calls are more expensive.

This is not a complete list of all possible question forms, although most of the others are variations of these common types. You will always get complete directions for answering questions. Be sure you understand *how* to mark your answers – ask questions until you do.

V. RECORDING YOUR ANSWERS

Computer terminals are used more and more today for many different kinds of exams.

For an examination with very few applicants, you may be told to record your answers in the test booklet itself. Separate answer sheets are much more common. If this separate answer sheet is to be scored by machine – and this is often the case – it is highly important that you mark your answers correctly in order to get credit.

An electronic scoring machine is often used in civil service offices because of the speed with which papers can be scored. Machine-scored answer sheets must be marked with a pencil, which will be given to you. This pencil has a high graphite content which responds to the electronic scoring machine. As a matter of fact, stray dots may register as answers, so do not let your pencil rest on the answer sheet while you are pondering the correct answer. Also, if your pencil lead breaks or is otherwise defective, ask for another.

Since the answer sheet will be dropped in a slot in the scoring machine, be careful not to bend the corners or get the paper crumpled.

The answer sheet normally has five vertical columns of numbers, with 30 numbers to a column. These numbers correspond to the question numbers in your test booklet. After each number, going across the page are four or five pairs of dotted lines. These short dotted lines have small letters or numbers above them. The first two pairs may also have a "T" or "F" above the letters. This indicates that the first two pairs only are to be used if the questions are of the true-false type. If the questions are multiple choice, disregard the "T" and "F" and pay attention only to the small letters or numbers.

Answer your questions in the manner of the sample that follows:

32. The largest city in the United States is
    A. Washington, D.C.
    B. New York City
    C. Chicago
    D. Detroit
    E. San Francisco

1) Choose the answer you think is best. (New York City is the largest, so "B" is correct.)
2) Find the row of dotted lines numbered the same as the question you are answering. (Find row number 32)
3) Find the pair of dotted lines corresponding to the answer. (Find the pair of lines under the mark "B.")
4) Make a solid black mark between the dotted lines.

VI. BEFORE THE TEST

Common sense will help you find procedures to follow to get ready for an examination. Too many of us, however, overlook these sensible measures. Indeed, nervousness and fatigue have been found to be the most serious reasons why applicants fail to do their best on civil service tests. Here is a list of reminders:

- Begin your preparation early – Don't wait until the last minute to go scurrying around for books and materials or to find out what the position is all about.
- Prepare continuously – An hour a night for a week is better than an all-night cram session. This has been definitely established. What is more, a night a week for a month will return better dividends than crowding your study into a shorter period of time.
- Locate the place of the exam – You have been sent a notice telling you when and where to report for the examination. If the location is in a different town or otherwise unfamiliar to you, it would be well to inquire the best route and learn something about the building.
- Relax the night before the test – Allow your mind to rest. Do not study at all that night. Plan some mild recreation or diversion; then go to bed early and get a good night's sleep.
- Get up early enough to make a leisurely trip to the place for the test – This way unforeseen events, traffic snarls, unfamiliar buildings, etc. will not upset you.
- Dress comfortably – A written test is not a fashion show. You will be known by number and not by name, so wear something comfortable.

- Leave excess paraphernalia at home – Shopping bags and odd bundles will get in your way. You need bring only the items mentioned in the official notice you received; usually everything you need is provided. Do not bring reference books to the exam. They will only confuse those last minutes and be taken away from you when in the test room.
- Arrive somewhat ahead of time – If because of transportation schedules you must get there very early, bring a newspaper or magazine to take your mind off yourself while waiting.
- Locate the examination room – When you have found the proper room, you will be directed to the seat or part of the room where you will sit. Sometimes you are given a sheet of instructions to read while you are waiting. Do not fill out any forms until you are told to do so; just read them and be prepared.
- Relax and prepare to listen to the instructions
- If you have any physical problem that may keep you from doing your best, be sure to tell the test administrator. If you are sick or in poor health, you really cannot do your best on the exam. You can come back and take the test some other time.

VII. AT THE TEST

The day of the test is here and you have the test booklet in your hand. The temptation to get going is very strong. Caution! There is more to success than knowing the right answers. You must know how to identify your papers and understand variations in the type of short-answer question used in this particular examination. Follow these suggestions for maximum results from your efforts:

1) Cooperate with the monitor

The test administrator has a duty to create a situation in which you can be as much at ease as possible. He will give instructions, tell you when to begin, check to see that you are marking your answer sheet correctly, and so on. He is not there to guard you, although he will see that your competitors do not take unfair advantage. He wants to help you do your best.

2) Listen to all instructions

Don't jump the gun! Wait until you understand all directions. In most civil service tests you get more time than you need to answer the questions. So don't be in a hurry. Read each word of instructions until you clearly understand the meaning. Study the examples, listen to all announcements and follow directions. Ask questions if you do not understand what to do.

3) Identify your papers

Civil service exams are usually identified by number only. You will be assigned a number; you must not put your name on your test papers. Be sure to copy your number correctly. Since more than one exam may be given, copy your exact examination title.

4) Plan your time

Unless you are told that a test is a "speed" or "rate of work" test, speed itself is usually not important. Time enough to answer all the questions will be provided, but this does not mean that you have all day. An overall time limit has been set. Divide the total time (in minutes) by the number of questions to determine the approximate time you have for each question.

5) Do not linger over difficult questions
If you come across a difficult question, mark it with a paper clip (useful to have along) and come back to it when you have been through the booklet. One caution if you do this – be sure to skip a number on your answer sheet as well. Check often to be sure that you have not lost your place and that you are marking in the row numbered the same as the question you are answering.

6) Read the questions
Be sure you know what the question asks! Many capable people are unsuccessful because they failed to *read* the questions correctly.

7) Answer all questions
Unless you have been instructed that a penalty will be deducted for incorrect answers, it is better to guess than to omit a question.

8) Speed tests
It is often better NOT to guess on speed tests. It has been found that on timed tests people are tempted to spend the last few seconds before time is called in marking answers at random – without even reading them – in the hope of picking up a few extra points. To discourage this practice, the instructions may warn you that your score will be "corrected" for guessing. That is, a penalty will be applied. The incorrect answers will be deducted from the correct ones, or some other penalty formula will be used.

9) Review your answers
If you finish before time is called, go back to the questions you guessed or omitted to give them further thought. Review other answers if you have time.

10) Return your test materials
If you are ready to leave before others have finished or time is called, take ALL your materials to the monitor and leave quietly. Never take any test material with you. The monitor can discover whose papers are not complete, and taking a test booklet may be grounds for disqualification.

VIII. EXAMINATION TECHNIQUES

1) Read the general instructions carefully. These are usually printed on the first page of the exam booklet. As a rule, these instructions refer to the timing of the examination; the fact that you should not start work until the signal and must stop work at a signal, etc. If there are any *special* instructions, such as a choice of questions to be answered, make sure that you note this instruction carefully.

2) When you are ready to start work on the examination, that is as soon as the signal has been given, read the instructions to each question booklet, underline any key words or phrases, such as *least, best, outline, describe* and the like. In this way you will tend to answer as requested rather than discover on reviewing your paper that you *listed without describing*, that you selected the *worst* choice rather than the *best* choice, etc.

3) If the examination is of the objective or multiple-choice type – that is, each question will also give a series of possible answers: A, B, C or D, and you are called upon to select the best answer and write the letter next to that answer on your answer paper – it is advisable to start answering each question in turn. There may be anywhere from 50 to 100 such questions in the three or four hours allotted and you can see how much time would be taken if you read through all the questions before beginning to answer any. Furthermore, if you come across a question or group of questions which you know would be difficult to answer, it would undoubtedly affect your handling of all the other questions.

4) If the examination is of the essay type and contains but a few questions, it is a moot point as to whether you should read all the questions before starting to answer any one. Of course, if you are given a choice – say five out of seven and the like – then it is essential to read all the questions so you can eliminate the two that are most difficult. If, however, you are asked to answer all the questions, there may be danger in trying to answer the easiest one first because you may find that you will spend too much time on it. The best technique is to answer the first question, then proceed to the second, etc.

5) Time your answers. Before the exam begins, write down the time it started, then add the time allowed for the examination and write down the time it must be completed, then divide the time available somewhat as follows:
   - If 3-1/2 hours are allowed, that would be 210 minutes. If you have 80 objective-type questions, that would be an average of 2-1/2 minutes per question. Allow yourself no more than 2 minutes per question, or a total of 160 minutes, which will permit about 50 minutes to review.
   - If for the time allotment of 210 minutes there are 7 essay questions to answer, that would average about 30 minutes a question. Give yourself only 25 minutes per question so that you have about 35 minutes to review.

6) The most important instruction is to *read each question* and make sure you know what is wanted. The second most important instruction is to *time yourself properly* so that you answer every question. The third most important instruction is to *answer every question*. Guess if you have to but include something for each question. Remember that you will receive no credit for a blank and will probably receive some credit if you write something in answer to an essay question. If you guess a letter – say "B" for a multiple-choice question – you may have guessed right. If you leave a blank as an answer to a multiple-choice question, the examiners may respect your feelings but it will not add a point to your score. Some exams may penalize you for wrong answers, so in such cases *only*, you may not want to guess unless you have some basis for your answer.

7) Suggestions
   a. Objective-type questions
      1. Examine the question booklet for proper sequence of pages and questions
      2. Read all instructions carefully
      3. Skip any question which seems too difficult; return to it after all other questions have been answered
      4. Apportion your time properly; do not spend too much time on any single question or group of questions

5. Note and underline key words – *all, most, fewest, least, best, worst, same, opposite*, etc.
6. Pay particular attention to negatives
7. Note unusual option, e.g., unduly long, short, complex, different or similar in content to the body of the question
8. Observe the use of "hedging" words – *probably, may, most likely*, etc.
9. Make sure that your answer is put next to the same number as the question
10. Do not second-guess unless you have good reason to believe the second answer is definitely more correct
11. Cross out original answer if you decide another answer is more accurate; do not erase until you are ready to hand your paper in
12. Answer all questions; guess unless instructed otherwise
13. Leave time for review

   b. Essay questions
      1. Read each question carefully
      2. Determine exactly what is wanted. Underline key words or phrases.
      3. Decide on outline or paragraph answer
      4. Include many different points and elements unless asked to develop any one or two points or elements
      5. Show impartiality by giving pros and cons unless directed to select one side only
      6. Make and write down any assumptions you find necessary to answer the questions
      7. Watch your English, grammar, punctuation and choice of words
      8. Time your answers; don't crowd material

8) Answering the essay question

Most essay questions can be answered by framing the specific response around several key words or ideas. Here are a few such key words or ideas:

M's: manpower, materials, methods, money, management
P's: purpose, program, policy, plan, procedure, practice, problems, pitfalls, personnel, public relations

   a. Six basic steps in handling problems:
      1. Preliminary plan and background development
      2. Collect information, data and facts
      3. Analyze and interpret information, data and facts
      4. Analyze and develop solutions as well as make recommendations
      5. Prepare report and sell recommendations
      6. Install recommendations and follow up effectiveness

   b. Pitfalls to avoid
      1. *Taking things for granted* – A statement of the situation does not necessarily imply that each of the elements is necessarily true; for example, a complaint may be invalid and biased so that all that can be taken for granted is that a complaint has been registered

2. *Considering only one side of a situation* – Wherever possible, indicate several alternatives and then point out the reasons you selected the best one
3. *Failing to indicate follow up* – Whenever your answer indicates action on your part, make certain that you will take proper follow-up action to see how successful your recommendations, procedures or actions turn out to be
4. *Taking too long in answering any single question* – Remember to time your answers properly

IX. AFTER THE TEST

Scoring procedures differ in detail among civil service jurisdictions although the general principles are the same. Whether the papers are hand-scored or graded by machine we have described, they are nearly always graded by number. That is, the person who marks the paper knows only the number – never the name – of the applicant. Not until all the papers have been graded will they be matched with names. If other tests, such as training and experience or oral interview ratings have been given, scores will be combined. Different parts of the examination usually have different weights. For example, the written test might count 60 percent of the final grade, and a rating of training and experience 40 percent. In many jurisdictions, veterans will have a certain number of points added to their grades.

After the final grade has been determined, the names are placed in grade order and an eligible list is established. There are various methods for resolving ties between those who get the same final grade – probably the most common is to place first the name of the person whose application was received first. Job offers are made from the eligible list in the order the names appear on it. You will be notified of your grade and your rank as soon as all these computations have been made. This will be done as rapidly as possible.

People who are found to meet the requirements in the announcement are called "eligibles." Their names are put on a list of eligible candidates. An eligible's chances of getting a job depend on how high he stands on this list and how fast agencies are filling jobs from the list.

When a job is to be filled from a list of eligibles, the agency asks for the names of people on the list of eligibles for that job. When the civil service commission receives this request, it sends to the agency the names of the three people highest on this list. Or, if the job to be filled has specialized requirements, the office sends the agency the names of the top three persons who meet these requirements from the general list.

The appointing officer makes a choice from among the three people whose names were sent to him. If the selected person accepts the appointment, the names of the others are put back on the list to be considered for future openings.

That is the rule in hiring from all kinds of eligible lists, whether they are for typist, carpenter, chemist, or something else. For every vacancy, the appointing officer has his choice of any one of the top three eligibles on the list. This explains why the person whose name is on top of the list sometimes does not get an appointment when some of the persons lower on the list do. If the appointing officer chooses the second or third eligible, the No. 1 eligible does not get a job at once, but stays on the list until he is appointed or the list is terminated.

X. HOW TO PASS THE INTERVIEW TEST

The examination for which you applied requires an oral interview test. You have already taken the written test and you are now being called for the interview test – the final part of the formal examination.

You may think that it is not possible to prepare for an interview test and that there are no procedures to follow during an interview. Our purpose is to point out some things you can do in advance that will help you and some good rules to follow and pitfalls to avoid while you are being interviewed.

What is an interview supposed to test?

The written examination is designed to test the technical knowledge and competence of the candidate; the oral is designed to evaluate intangible qualities, not readily measured otherwise, and to establish a list showing the relative fitness of each candidate – as measured against his competitors – for the position sought. Scoring is not on the basis of "right" and "wrong," but on a sliding scale of values ranging from "not passable" to "outstanding." As a matter of fact, it is possible to achieve a relatively low score without a single "incorrect" answer because of evident weakness in the qualities being measured.

Occasionally, an examination may consist entirely of an oral test – either an individual or a group oral. In such cases, information is sought concerning the technical knowledges and abilities of the candidate, since there has been no written examination for this purpose. More commonly, however, an oral test is used to supplement a written examination.

Who conducts interviews?

The composition of oral boards varies among different jurisdictions. In nearly all, a representative of the personnel department serves as chairman. One of the members of the board may be a representative of the department in which the candidate would work. In some cases, "outside experts" are used, and, frequently, a businessman or some other representative of the general public is asked to serve. Labor and management or other special groups may be represented. The aim is to secure the services of experts in the appropriate field.

However the board is composed, it is a good idea (and not at all improper or unethical) to ascertain in advance of the interview who the members are and what groups they represent. When you are introduced to them, you will have some idea of their backgrounds and interests, and at least you will not stutter and stammer over their names.

What should be done before the interview?

While knowledge about the board members is useful and takes some of the surprise element out of the interview, there is other preparation which is more substantive. It *is* possible to prepare for an oral interview – in several ways:

1) Keep a copy of your application and review it carefully before the interview

This may be the only document before the oral board, and the starting point of the interview. Know what education and experience you have listed there, and the sequence and dates of all of it. Sometimes the board will ask you to review the highlights of your experience for them; you should not have to hem and haw doing it.

2) Study the class specification and the examination announcement

Usually, the oral board has one or both of these to guide them. The qualities, characteristics or knowledges required by the position sought are stated in these documents. They offer valuable clues as to the nature of the oral interview. For example, if the job involves supervisory responsibilities, the announcement will usually indicate that knowledge of modern supervisory methods and the qualifications of the candidate as a supervisor will be tested. If so, you can expect such questions, frequently in the form of a hypothetical situation which you are expected to solve. NEVER go into an oral without knowledge of the duties and responsibilities of the job you seek.

3) Think through each qualification required

Try to visualize the kind of questions you would ask if you were a board member. How well could you answer them? Try especially to appraise your own knowledge and background in each area, *measured against the job sought*, and identify any areas in which you are weak. Be critical and realistic – do not flatter yourself.

4) Do some general reading in areas in which you feel you may be weak

For example, if the job involves supervision and your past experience has NOT, some general reading in supervisory methods and practices, particularly in the field of human relations, might be useful. Do NOT study agency procedures or detailed manuals. The oral board will be testing your understanding and capacity, not your memory.

5) Get a good night's sleep and watch your general health and mental attitude

You will want a clear head at the interview. Take care of a cold or any other minor ailment, and of course, no hangovers.

What should be done on the day of the interview?

Now comes the day of the interview itself. Give yourself plenty of time to get there. Plan to arrive somewhat ahead of the scheduled time, particularly if your appointment is in the fore part of the day. If a previous candidate fails to appear, the board might be ready for you a bit early. By early afternoon an oral board is almost invariably behind schedule if there are many candidates, and you may have to wait. Take along a book or magazine to read, or your application to review, but leave any extraneous material in the waiting room when you go in for your interview. In any event, relax and compose yourself.

The matter of dress is important. The board is forming impressions about you – from your experience, your manners, your attitude, and your appearance. Give your personal appearance careful attention. Dress your best, but not your flashiest. Choose conservative, appropriate clothing, and be sure it is immaculate. This is a business interview, and your appearance should indicate that you regard it as such. Besides, being well groomed and properly dressed will help boost your confidence.

Sooner or later, someone will call your name and escort you into the interview room. *This is it.* From here on you are on your own. It is too late for any more preparation. But remember, you asked for this opportunity to prove your fitness, and you are here because your request was granted.

What happens when you go in?

The usual sequence of events will be as follows: The clerk (who is often the board stenographer) will introduce you to the chairman of the oral board, who will introduce you to the other members of the board. Acknowledge the introductions before you sit down. Do not be surprised if you find a microphone facing you or a stenotypist sitting by. Oral interviews are usually recorded in the event of an appeal or other review.

Usually the chairman of the board will open the interview by reviewing the highlights of your education and work experience from your application – primarily for the benefit of the other members of the board, as well as to get the material into the record. Do not interrupt or comment unless there is an error or significant misinterpretation; if that is the case, do not hesitate. But do not quibble about insignificant matters. Also, he will usually ask you some question about your education, experience or your present job – partly to get you to start talking and to establish the interviewing "rapport." He may start the actual questioning, or turn it over to one of the other members. Frequently, each member undertakes the questioning on a particular area, one in which he is perhaps most competent, so you can expect each member to participate in the examination. Because time is limited, you may also expect some rather abrupt switches in the direction the questioning takes, so do not be upset by it. Normally, a board member will not pursue a single line of questioning unless he discovers a particular strength or weakness.

After each member has participated, the chairman will usually ask whether any member has any further questions, then will ask you if you have anything you wish to add. Unless you are expecting this question, it may floor you. Worse, it may start you off on an extended, extemporaneous speech. The board is not usually seeking more information. The question is principally to offer you a last opportunity to present further qualifications or to indicate that you have nothing to add. So, if you feel that a significant qualification or characteristic has been overlooked, it is proper to point it out in a sentence or so. Do not compliment the board on the thoroughness of their examination – they have been sketchy, and you know it. If you wish, merely say, "No thank you, I have nothing further to add." This is a point where you can "talk yourself out" of a good impression or fail to present an important bit of information. Remember, *you close the interview yourself.*

The chairman will then say, "That is all, Mr. _____, thank you." Do not be startled; the interview is over, and quicker than you think. Thank him, gather your belongings and take your leave. Save your sigh of relief for the other side of the door.

How to put your best foot forward
Throughout this entire process, you may feel that the board individually and collectively is trying to pierce your defenses, seek out your hidden weaknesses and embarrass and confuse you. Actually, this is not true. They are obliged to make an appraisal of your qualifications for the job you are seeking, and they want to see you in your best light. Remember, they must interview all candidates and a non-cooperative candidate may become a failure in spite of their best efforts to bring out his qualifications. Here are 15 suggestions that will help you:

1) Be natural – Keep your attitude confident, not cocky
If you are not confident that you can do the job, do not expect the board to be. Do not apologize for your weaknesses, try to bring out your strong points. The board is interested in a positive, not negative, presentation. Cockiness will antagonize any board member and make him wonder if you are covering up a weakness by a false show of strength.

2) Get comfortable, but don't lounge or sprawl
Sit erectly but not stiffly. A careless posture may lead the board to conclude that you are careless in other things, or at least that you are not impressed by the importance of the occasion. Either conclusion is natural, even if incorrect. Do not fuss with your clothing, a pencil or an ashtray. Your hands may occasionally be useful to emphasize a point; do not let them become a point of distraction.

3) Do not wisecrack or make small talk
This is a serious situation, and your attitude should show that you consider it as such. Further, the time of the board is limited – they do not want to waste it, and neither should you.

4) Do not exaggerate your experience or abilities
In the first place, from information in the application or other interviews and sources, the board may know more about you than you think. Secondly, you probably will not get away with it. An experienced board is rather adept at spotting such a situation, so do not take the chance.

5) If you know a board member, do not make a point of it, yet do not hide it
Certainly you are not fooling him, and probably not the other members of the board. Do not try to take advantage of your acquaintanceship – it will probably do you little good.

6) Do not dominate the interview
Let the board do that. They will give you the clues – do not assume that you have to do all the talking. Realize that the board has a number of questions to ask you, and do not try to take up all the interview time by showing off your extensive knowledge of the answer to the first one.

7) Be attentive
You only have 20 minutes or so, and you should keep your attention at its sharpest throughout. When a member is addressing a problem or question to you, give him your undivided attention. Address your reply principally to him, but do not exclude the other board members.

8) Do not interrupt
A board member may be stating a problem for you to analyze. He will ask you a question when the time comes. Let him state the problem, and wait for the question.

9) Make sure you understand the question
Do not try to answer until you are sure what the question is. If it is not clear, restate it in your own words or ask the board member to clarify it for you. However, do not haggle about minor elements.

10) Reply promptly but not hastily
A common entry on oral board rating sheets is "candidate responded readily," or "candidate hesitated in replies." Respond as promptly and quickly as you can, but do not jump to a hasty, ill-considered answer.

11) Do not be peremptory in your answers
A brief answer is proper – but do not fire your answer back. That is a losing game from your point of view. The board member can probably ask questions much faster than you can answer them.

12) Do not try to create the answer you think the board member wants
He is interested in what kind of mind you have and how it works – not in playing games. Furthermore, he can usually spot this practice and will actually grade you down on it.

13) Do not switch sides in your reply merely to agree with a board member
Frequently, a member will take a contrary position merely to draw you out and to see if you are willing and able to defend your point of view. Do not start a debate, yet do not surrender a good position. If a position is worth taking, it is worth defending.

14) Do not be afraid to admit an error in judgment if you are shown to be wrong

The board knows that you are forced to reply without any opportunity for careful consideration. Your answer may be demonstrably wrong. If so, admit it and get on with the interview.

15) Do not dwell at length on your present job

The opening question may relate to your present assignment. Answer the question but do not go into an extended discussion. You are being examined for a *new* job, not your present one. As a matter of fact, try to phrase ALL your answers in terms of the job for which you are being examined.

Basis of Rating

Probably you will forget most of these "do's" and "don'ts" when you walk into the oral interview room. Even remembering them all will not ensure you a passing grade. Perhaps you did not have the qualifications in the first place. But remembering them will help you to put your best foot forward, without treading on the toes of the board members.

Rumor and popular opinion to the contrary notwithstanding, an oral board wants you to make the best appearance possible. They know you are under pressure – but they also want to see how you respond to it as a guide to what your reaction would be under the pressures of the job you seek. They will be influenced by the degree of poise you display, the personal traits you show and the manner in which you respond.

ABOUT THIS BOOK

This book contains tests divided into Examination Sections. Go through each test, answering every question in the margin. We have also attached a sample answer sheet at the back of the book that can be removed and used. At the end of each test look at the answer key and check your answers. On the ones you got wrong, look at the right answer choice and learn. Do not fill in the answers first. Do not memorize the questions and answers, but understand the answer and principles involved. On your test, the questions will likely be different from the samples. Questions are changed and new ones added. If you understand these past questions you should have success with any changes that arise. Tests may consist of several types of questions. We have additional books on each subject should more study be advisable or necessary for you. Finally, the more you study, the better prepared you will be. This book is intended to be the last thing you study before you walk into the examination room. Prior study of relevant texts is also recommended. NLC publishes some of these in our Fundamental Series. Knowledge and good sense are important factors in passing your exam. Good luck also helps. So now study this Passbook, absorb the material contained within and take that knowledge into the examination. Then do your best to pass that exam.

EXAMINATION SECTION

EXAMINATION SECTION
TEST 1

Memory for Addresses Test

DIRECTIONS: In this test you will have to memorize the locations (A, B, C, D or E) of 25 addresses shown in five boxes. For example, "Sardis" is in box "C," "4300-4799 West" is in box "E," etc. Study the locations of the addresses for five minutes (try sounding them to yourself), then cover the boxes and try to answer the questions below. *PRINT THE LETTER OF THE CORRECT ANSWER IN THE SPACE AT THE RIGHT.*

Box A	Box B	Box C
4700-5599 Table	6800-6999 Table	5600-6499 Table
Lismore	Kelford	Joel
4800-5199 West	5200-5799 West	3200-3499 West
Hesper	Musella	Sardis
5500-6399 Blake	4800-5499 Blake	6400-7299 Blake

BoxD	BoxE
6500-6799 Table	4400-4699 Table
Tatum	Ruskin
3500-4299 West	4300-4799 West
Porter	Somers
4300-4799 Blake	7300-7499 Blake

1. Musella   1.____
2. 4300-4799 Blake   2.____
3. 4700-5599 Table   3.____
4. Tatum   4.____
5. 5500-6399 Blake   5.____
6. Hesper   6.____
7. Kelford   7.____
8. Somers   8.____
9. 6400-7299 Blake   9.____
10. Joel   10.____
11. 5500-6399 Blake   11.____
12. 5200-5799 West   12.____
13. Porter   13.____
14. 7300-7499 Blake   14.____

KEY (CORRECT ANSWERS)

1. B
2. D
3. A
4. D
5. A
6. A
7. B
8. E
9. C
10. C
11. A
12. B
13. D
14. E

TEST 2

Address Checking Test

DIRECTIONS: In this test you will have to decide whether two addresses are alike or different. If the two addresses are exactly alike in every way, mark the answer "A." If the two addresses are different, mark the answer "D." *PRINT THE LETTER OF THE CORRECT ANSWER IN THE SPACE AT THE RIGHT.*

1. 2134 S. 20th St.   2134 S. 20th St.   1.____
2. 4608 N. Warnock St.   4806 N. Warnock St.   2.____
3. 1202 W. Girard Dr.   1202 W. Girard Rd.   3.____
4. Chappaqua, NY 10514   Chappaqua, NY 10514   4.____
5. 2207 Markland Ave.   2207 Markham Ave.   5.____

General Test

DIRECTIONS: In this test there are three kinds of questions—Vocabulary, Reading and Number Series. For Vocabulary questions, like number 6, choose the suggested answer that means most nearly the same as the word or words in italics. For Reading questions, like number 7, read the paragraph and answer the question that follows it. For Number Series questions, like numbers 8 through 25, there is a series of numbers which is arranged in some definite order or pattern, followed by five sets of two numbers each. Determine the order or pattern of the numbers at the left and choose from the selections below the two numbers that would properly continue the order or pattern. *PRINT THE LETTER OF THE CORRECT ANSWER IN THE SPACE AT THE RIGHT.*

6. The reports were *consolidated by* the secretary. *Consolidated* most nearly means   6.____

    A. combined   B. concluded   C. distributed   D. protected   E. weighed

7. "Post office clerks assigned to stamp windows are directly responsible financially in the selling of postage. In addition, they are expected to have a thorough knowledge as to the acceptability of matter offered for mailing. Any information which they give out to the public must be accurate."   7.____

   The paragraph best supports the statement that clerks assigned to stamp-window duty

    A. must account for stamps issued to them for sale
    B. have had long training in other post-office work
    C. advise the public only on matters of official business
    D. must refer continuously to the sources of postal regulations
    E. inspect the contents of every package offered for mailing

8. 1 2 3 4 5 6 7 ...   8.____

    A. 1 2   B. 5 6   C. 8 9
    D. 4 5   E. 7 8

9. 15 14 13 12 11 10 9 ...
   A. 2 1
   B. 17 16
   C. 8 9
   D. 8 7
   E. 9 8

10. 20 20 21 21 22 22 23 ...
    A. 23 23
    B. 23 24
    C. 19 19
    D. 22 23
    E. 21 22

11. 17 3 17 4 17 5 17 ...
    A. 6 17
    B. 6 7
    C. 17 6
    D. 5 6
    E. 17 7

12. 1 2 4 5 7 8 10 ...
    A. 11 12
    B. 12 14
    C. 10 13
    D. 12 13
    E. 11 13

13. 21 21 20 20 19 19 18 ...
    A. 18 18
    B. 18 17
    C. 17 18
    D. 17 17
    E. 18 19

14. 1 22 1 23 1 24 1 ...
    A. 26 1
    B. 25 26
    C. 25 1
    D. 1 26
    E. 1 25

15. 1 20 3 19 5 18 7 ...
    A. 8 9
    B. 8 17
    C. 17 10
    D. 17 9
    E. 9 18

16. 4 7 10 13 16 19 22 ...
    A. 23 26
    B. 25 27
    C. 25 26
    D. 25 28
    E. 24 27

17. 30 2 28 4 26 6 24 ...
    A. 23 9
    B. 26 8
    C. 8 9
    D. 26 22
    E. 8 22

18. 5 6 20 7 8 19 9 ...
    A. 10 18
    B. 18 17
    C. 10 7
    D. 18 19
    E. 10 11

19. 9 10 1 11 12 2 13 ...
    A. 2 14
    B. 3 14
    C. 14 3
    D. 14 15
    E. 14 1

20. 4 6 9 11 14 16 19 ...
    A. 21 24
    B. 22 25
    C. 20 22
    D. 21 23
    E. 22 24

21. 8 8 1 10 10 3 12 ...

    A. 13 13   B. 12 5   C. 12 4
    D. 13 5   E. 4 12

22. 14 1 2 15 3 4 16...

    A. 5 16   B. 6 7   C. 5 17
    D. 5 6   E. 17 5

23. 10 12 50 15 17 50 20 ...

    A. 50 21   B. 21 50   C. 50 22
    D. 22 50   E. 22 24

24. 1 2 3 50 4 5 6 51 7 8...

    A. 9 10   B. 9 52   C. 51 10
    D. 10 52   E. 10 50

25. 20 21 23 24 27 28 32 33 38 39 ...

    A. 45 46   B. 45 52   C. 44 45
    D. 44 49   E. 40 46

KEY (CORRECT ANSWERS)

1. A
2. D
3. D
4. A
5. D

6. A
7. A
8. C
9. D
10. B

11. A
12. E
13. B
14. C
15. D

16. D
17. E
18. A
19. C
20. A

21. B
22. D
23. D
24. B
25. A

Address Checking

DESCRIPTION OF THE TEST AND SAMPLE QUESTIONS

Every member of the Postal work force is responsible for seeing that every letter reaches the right address. If one worker makes an error in reading an address, it can cause a serious delay in getting the letter to where it is supposed to go.

Both the Clerk-Carrier and Mail Handler examinations include tests of address checking. The test in the Clerk-Carrier examination is harder than the one in the Mail Handler examination. The Mail Handler test has only names of cities and states with some zip codes, while the Clerk-Carrier test has street addresses also.

Can you spot whether or not two addresses are alike or different? It is as easy as that. But how fast can you do it accurately? Look at the sample questions below. Each question consists of a pair of addresses like this—

762 W 18th St   762 W 18th St
    Are they Alike or Different? They are exactly Alike.
9486 Hillsdale Rd   9489 Hillsdale Rd
    Alike or Different? They are Different. Do you see why?
1242 RegalSt   1242 Regel St
    Alike or Different?

Remember that this test measures both speed and accuracy. So work as fast as you can without making any mistakes. Have a friend time you while you are working on the practice tests—you may find that you get faster as you become used to this type of question.

Hints for Answering Address-Checking Questions
- Do not spend too much time on any one question.
- The difference may not be noticeable at first, so be sure to check
  —all numbers (are they alike and in the same order or are they different)
  —abbreviations, such as St, Rd, NW, N Y (are they alike or are they different)
  —spellings of street, city, and state names
- Do not get nervous about the time limit. (In the official test no one is expected to do all the questions in the time allowed.)
- Make sure that you have marked the correct box for each question.

Address Checking—Sample Questions

Starting now, if the two addresses are ALIKE darken box A on the Sample Answer Sheet below. If the two addresses are DIFFERENT in any way darken box D. Answer every question.

1 ... 239 Windell Ave   239 Windell Ave
   Alike or Different? Alike. Mark space A for question 1.
2 ... 4667 Edgeworth Rd   4677 Edgeworth Rd
   Alike or Different? Different. Mark space D for question 2.
3 ... 2661 Kennel St SE   2661 Kennel St SW
4 ... 3709 Columbine St   3707 Columbine St
5 ... 969 W 14th St NW   969 W 14th St NW
6 ... 4439 Frederick Pkwy   4439 Frederick Pkwy
7 ... 77 Summers St   77 Summers St
8 ... 828 N Franklin Pl   828 S Franklin Pl

Check your answers with the correct answers. If you have any wrong answers, be sure you see why before you go on.

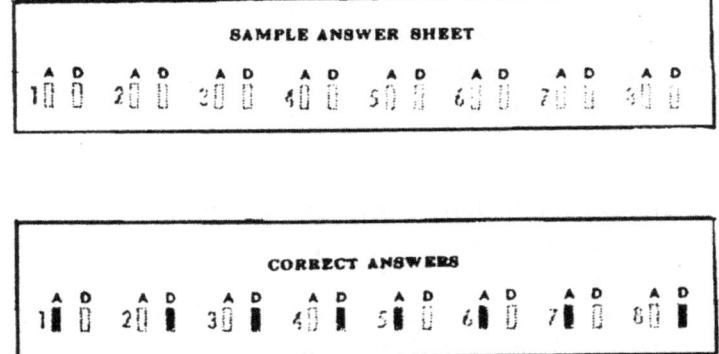

The addresses in the Practice Tests are like the ones you will have to check in the examinations. The ones in Practice Test 1 are like the ones in the Mail Handler examination. Work as fast as you can, but be careful because you will lose points for making mistakes. Be sure to take no more than the correct time for each test. Check your answers with the answers at the end of each test.

Now turn the page and take the first Practice Test.

ADDRESS CHECKING—PRACTICE TEST 1

Work exactly *3 minutes*. No more. No less. If you finish before the 3 minutes are up, go over your answers again. Be sure to mark your answers on the Sample Answer Sheet on the next page.

1 ...	Purdin Mo	Purdon Mo
2 ...	Hobart Ind 46342	Hobart Ind 46342
3 ...	Kuna Idaho	Kuna Idaho
4 ...	Janesville Calif 96114	Janesville Calif 96119
5 ...	Sioux Falls S Dak	Sioux Falls S Dak
6 ...	Homewood Miss	Homewood Miss
7 ...	Kaweah Calif	Kawaeh Calif
8 ...	Unionport Ohio	Unionport Ohio
9 ...	Meyersdale Pa	Meyersdale Va
10 ...	Coquille Oreg 97423	Coqville Oreg 97423
11 ...	Milan Wis	Milam Wis
12 ...	Prospect Ky	Prospect Ky
13 ...	Cloversville N Y	Cloverville N Y
14 ...	Locate Mont 59340	Locate Mont 59340
15 ...	Bozman Md	Bozeman Md
16 ...	Orient Ill	Orient Ill
17 ...	Yosemite Ky 42566	Yosemite Ky 42566
18 ...	Camden Miss 39045	Camden Miss 39054
19 ...	Bennington Vt	Bennington Vt
20 ...	La Farge Wis	La Farge Wis
21 ...	Fairfield N Y	Fairfield N C
22 ...	Wynot Nebr	Wynot Nebr
23 ...	Arona Pa	Aroda Pa
24 ...	Thurman N C 28683	Thurmond N C 28683
25 ...	Zenda Kans	Zenba Kans
26 ...	Pike N H	Pike N H
27 ...	Gorst Wash 98337	Gorst Wash 98837
28 ...	Joiner Ark	Joiner Ark
29 ...	Normangee Tex	Normangee Tex
30 ...	Toccoa Ga	Tococa Ga
31 ...	Small Point Maine 04567	Small Point Maine 04567
32 ...	Eagan Tenn	Eagar Tenn
33 ...	Belfield N Dak	Belford N Dak
34 ...	De Ridder La 70634	De Ridder La 70634
35 ...	Van Meter Iowa	Van Meter Iowa
36 ...	Valparaiso Fla	Valparaiso Ind
37 ...	Souris N Dak	Souris N Dak
38 ...	Robbinston Maine	Robbinstown Maine
39 ...	Dawes W Va 25054	Dawes W Va 25054
40 ...	Goltry Okla	Goltrey Okla

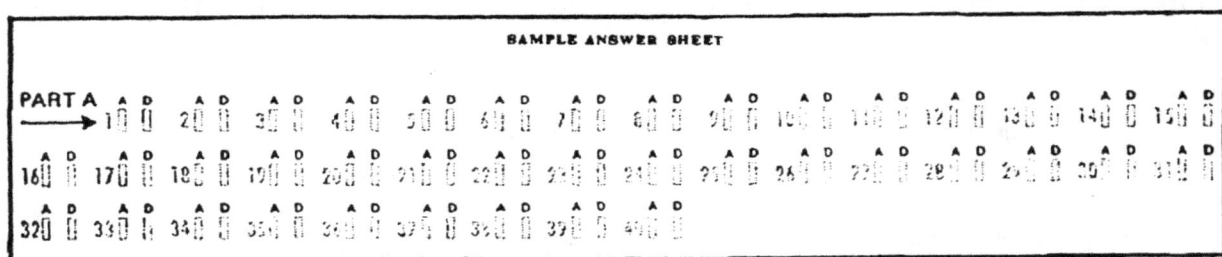

Now check your answers by comparing your answers with the correct answers shown below.

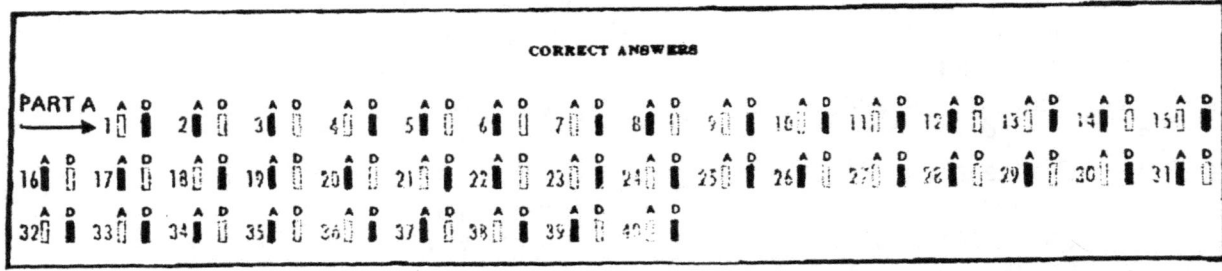

Count how many you got right, and write that number on this line─────────────────────────────▶ Number Right ─────

Now count how many you got wrong, and write that number on this line─────────────────────────────▶ Number Wrong ═════

Subtract the Number Wrong from the Number Right and write the Difference on this line─────────────────▶ Total Score ─────

Meaning of Test Score

If your Total Score is *26 or more,* you have a Good score.

If your Total Score is from *16 to 25,* you have a Fair score.

If your Total Score is *15 or less,* you are not doing too well.

You may be going too slowly, or you may be making too many mistakes. You need more practice.

ADDRESS CHECKING—PRACTICE TEST 2

These addresses are a little harder.

Remember to work as fast as you can but be careful. Work exactly *3 minutes*. No more. No less. If you finish before the 3 minutes are up, go over your answers again. Be sure to mark your answers on the Sample Answer Sheet on the next page.

1 ...	7961 Eastern Ave SE	7961 Eastern Ave SE
2 ...	3809 20th Rd N	3309 20th Rd N
3 ...	Smicksburg Pa	Smithsburg Pa
4 ...	Sherman Conn	Sherman Conn
5 ...	Richland Ga	Richland La
6 ...	8520 Leesburg Pike SE	8520 Leesburg Pike SE
7 ...	Genevia Ark	Geneva Ark
8 ...	104 W Jefferson St	104 W Jefferson St
9 ...	Meandor WVa	Meander W Va
10 ...	6327 W Mari Ct	6327 W Mari Ct
11 ...	3191 Draper Dr SE	3191 Draper Dr SW
12 ...	1415 W Green Spring Rd	1415 W Green Spring Rd
13 ...	Parr Ind	Parr Ind
14 ...	East Falmouth Mass 02536	East Falmouth Miss 02536
15 ...	3016 N St NW	3016 M St NW
16 ...	Yukon Mo	Yukon Mo
17 ...	7057 Brookfield Plaza	7057 Brookfield Plaza
18 ...	Bethel Ohio 45106	Bethel Ohio 45106
19 ...	Littleton N H	Littleton N C
20 ...	8909 Bowie Dr	8909 Bowie Dr
21 ...	Colmar I11	Colmar I11
22 ...	784 Matthews Dr NE	784 Matthews Dr NE
23 ...	2923 John Marshall Dr	2932 John Marshall Dr
24 ...	6023 Woodmont Rd	6023 Woodmount Rd
25 ...	Nolan Tex	Noland Tex
26 ...	342 E Lincolnia Rd	342 E Lincolnia Dr
27 ...	Jane Calif	Jane Calif
28 ...	4921 Seminary Rd	4912 Seminary Rd
29 ...	Ulmers S C	Ullmers S C
30 ...	4804 Montgomery Lane SW	4804 Montgomery Lane SW
31 ...	210 E Fairfax Dr	210 W Fairfax Dr
32 ...	Hanapepe Hawaii	Hanapepe Hawaii
33 ...	450 La Calle del Punto	450 La Calle del Punto
34 ...	Walland Tenn 37886	Walland Tenn 37836
35 ...	Villamont Va	Villamont Va
36 ...	4102 Georgia Ave NW	4102 Georgia Rd NW
37 ...	Aroch Oreg	Aroch Oreg
38 ...	6531 N Walton Ave	6531 N Waldon Ave
39 ...	Jeff Ky	Jeff Ky
40 ...	Delphos Iowa	Delphis Iowa

SAMPLE ANSWER SHEET

PART A 1–40 (sample markings)

Now check your answers by comparing your answers with the correct answers shown below.

CORRECT ANSWERS

PART A 1–40 (correct markings)

Count how many you got right, and write that number on this line ⟶ Number Right _____

Now count how many you got wrong, and write that number on this line ⟶ Number Wrong _____

Subtract the Number Wrong from the Number Right and write the Difference on this line ⟶ Total Score _____

Meaning of Test Score

If your Total Score is *26 or more,* you have a Good score.

If your Total Score is from *16 to 25,* you have a Fair score.

If your Total Score is *15 or less,* you are not doing too well.

You may be going too slowly, or you may be making too many mistakes. You need more practice.

ADDRESS CHECKING-PRACTICE TEST 3

These addresses are exactly like the ones in the Clerk-Carrier examination. Even if you don't plan to take the Clerk-Carrier examination, this is good practice for the Mail Handler one. Work as fast as you can without making too many errors. Work exactly *3 minutes*. No more. No less. If you finish before the 3 minutes are up, go over your answers again. Mark your answers on the Sample Answer Sheet on the next page.

1 ...	2134 S 20th St	2134 S 20th St
2 ...	4608 N Warnock St	4806 N Warnock St
3 ...	1202 W Girard Dr	1202 W Girard Rd
4 ...	3120 S Harcourt St	3120 S Harcourt St
5 ...	4618 W Addison St	4618 E Addison St
6 ...	Sessums Miss	Sessoms Miss
7 ...	6425 N Delancey	6425 N Delancey
8 ...	5407 Columbia Rd	5407 Columbia Rd
9 ...	2106 Southern Ave	2106 Southern Ave
10 ...	Highfalls N C 27259	Highlands NC 27259
11 ...	2873 Pershing Dr	2873 Pershing Dr
12 ...	1329 N H Ave NW	1329 N J Ave NW
13 ...	1316 N Quinn St	1316 N Quinn St
14 ...	7507 Wyngate Dr	7505 Wyngate Dr
15 ...	2918 Colesville Rd	2918 Colesvale Rd
16 ...	2071 E Belvedere Dr	2071 E Belvedere Dr
17 ...	Palmer Wash	Palmer Mich
18 ...	2106 16th St SW	2106 16th St SW
19 ...	2207 Markland Ave	2207 Markham Ave
20 ...	5345 16th St SW	5345 16th St SE
21 ...	239 Summit Pl NE	239 Summit Pl NE
22 ...	152 Continental Pkwy	152 Continental Blvd
23 ...	8092 13th Rd S	8029 13th Rd S
24 ...	3906 Queensbury Rd	3906 Queensbury Rd
25 ...	4719 Linnean Ave NW	4719 Linnean Ave NE
26 ...	Bradford Me	Bradley Me
27 ...	Parrott Ga 31777	Parrott Ga 31177
28 ...	4312 Lowell Lane	4312 Lowell Lane
29 ...	6929 W 135th Place	6929 W 135th Plaza
30 ...	5143 Somerset Cir	5143 Somerset Cir
31 ...	8501 Kennedy St	8501 Kennedy St
32 ...	2164 E McLean Ave	2164 E McLean Ave
33 ...	7186 E St NW	7186 F St NW
34 ...	2121 Beechcrest Rd	2121 Beechcroft Rd
35 ...	3609 E Montrose St	3609 E Montrose St
36 ...	324 S Alvadero St	324 S Alverado St
37 ...	2908 Plaza de las Estrellas	2908 Plaza de las Estrellas
38 ...	223 Great Falls Rd SE	223 Great Falls Dr SE
39 ...	Kelton S C 29354	Kelton S C 29354
40 ...	3201 Landover Rd	3201 Landover Rd

```
                              SAMPLE ANSWER SHEET
PART A   A D   A D   A D   A D   A D   A D   A D   A D   A D   A D   A D   A D   A D   A D   A
──────▶
```

Now check your answers by comparing your answers with the correct answers shown below.

```
                              CORRECT ANSWERS
PART A   A D   A D   A D   A D   A D   A D   A D   A D   A D   A D   A D   A D   A D   A D   A D
──────▶ 1     2     3     4     5     6     7     8     9    10    11    12    13    14    15
        16    17    18    19    20    21    22    23    24    25    26    27    28    29    30
        31    32    33    34    35    36    37    38    39    40
```

Count how many you got right, and write that number on this
line ─────────────────────────────────▶ Number Right ─────
Now count how many you got wrong, and write that number on
this line ─────────────────────────────▶ Number Wrong ─────
Subtract the Number Wrong from the Number Right and write
the Difference on this line ─────────────────▶ Total Score ─────

Meaning of Test Score.
    If your Total Score is *26 or more,* you have a Good score.
    If your Total Score is from *16 to 25,* you have a Fair score.
    If your Total Score is *15 or less,* you are not doing too well.
        You may be going too slowly, or you may be making too many mistakes. You need
        more practice.

ADDRESS CHECKING

EXAMINATION SECTION
TEST 1

DIRECTIONS: This test is designed to measure your speed and accuracy. You are urged to work both quickly and accurately and to do correctly as many lists as you can in the time allowed. In this part, you will be given addresses to compare. If the two addresses are exactly <u>alike</u> in every way, circle the letter A. If the two addresses are <u>different</u> in any way, circle the letter D.

CIRCLE CORRECT ANSWER

1.	Purdin Mo	Purdon Mo	A	D
2.	Hobart In 46342	Hobart In 46342	A	D
3.	Kuna Id	Kuna Id	A	D
4.	Janesville Ca 96114	Kanesville Ca 96119	A	D
5.	Sioux Falls SD	Sioux Falls SD	A	D
6.	Homewood Ms	Homewood Ms	A	D
7.	Kaweah Ca	Kawaeh Ca	A	D
8.	Unionport Oh	Unionport Oh	A	D
9.	Meyersdale Pa	Meyersdale Va	A	D
10.	Coquille Or 97423	Coqville Or 97423	A	D
11.	Milan Wi	Milam Wi	A	D
12.	Prospect Ky	Prospect Ky	A	D
13.	Cloversville NY	Cloverville NY	A	D
14.	Locate Mt 59340	Locate Mt 59340	A	D
15.	Bozman Md	Bozeman Md	A	D
16.	Orient Il	Orient Il	A	D
17.	Yosemite Ky 42566	Yosemite Ky 42566	A	D
18.	Camden Ms 39045	Camden Ms 39054	A	D
19.	Bennington Vt	Bennington Vt	A	D
20.	La Farge Wi	La Farge Wi	A	D

KEY (CORRECT ANSWERS)

1.	D	11.	D
2.	A	12.	A
3.	A	13.	D
4.	D	14.	A
5.	A	15.	D
6.	A	16.	A
7.	D	17.	A
8.	A	18.	D
9.	D	19.	A
10.	D	20.	A

TEST 2

DIRECTIONS: This test is designed to measure your speed and accuracy. You are urged to work both quickly and accurately and to do correctly as many lists as you can in the time allowed. In this part, you will be given addresses to compare. If the two addresses are exactly <u>alike</u> in every way, circle the letter A. If the two addresses are <u>different</u> in any way, circle the letter D.

CIRCLE CORRECT ANSWER

1.	Fairfield NY	Fairfield NC	A	D
2.	Wynot Ne	Wynot Ne	A	D
3.	Arona Pa	Aroda Pa	A	D
4.	Thurman NC 28683	Thurmond NC 28683	A	D
5.	Zenda Ks	Zenba Ks	A	D
6.	Pike NH	Pike NH	A	D
7.	Gorst Wa 98337	Gorst Wa 98837	A	D
8.	Joiner Ar	Joiner Ar	A	D
9.	Normangee Tx	Mormangee Tx	A	D
10.	Taccoa Ga	Tococa Ga	A	D
11.	Small Point Me 04567	Small Point Me 04567	A	D
12.	Eagan Tn	Eagar Tn	A	D
13.	Belfield ND	Belford ND	A	D
14.	DeRidder La 70634	DeRidder La 70634	A	D
15.	Van Meter Ia	Van Meter Ia	A	D
16.	Valparaiso Fl	Valparaiso In	A	D
17.	Souris ND	Souris ND	A	D
18.	Robbinston Me	Robbinstown Me	A	D
19.	Dawes WV 25054	Dawes WV 25054	A	D
20.	Goltry Ok	Goultrey Ok	A	D

KEY (CORRECT ANSWERS)

1.	D	11.	A
2.	A	12.	D
3.	D	13.	D
4.	D	14.	A
5.	D	15.	A
6.	A	16.	D
7.	D	17.	A
8.	A	18.	D
9.	D	19.	A
10.	D	20.	D

TEST 3

DIRECTIONS: This test is designed to measure your speed and accuracy. You are urged to work both quickly and accurately and to do correctly as many lists as you can in the time allowed. In this part, you will be given addresses to compare. If the two addresses are exactly <u>alike</u> in every way, circle the letter A. If the two addresses are <u>different</u> in any way, circle the letter D.

CIRCLE
CORRECT ANSWER

1.	Las Vegas Nv	Las Vegas NM	A	D
2.	New Sarpy La	New Sarpy La	A	D
3.	Loma Mt	Loma Mt	A	D
4.	Pitsburg Oh	Pitsburg Oh	A	D
5.	Bloomington In	Bloomingdale In	A	D
6.	Eastabuchie Ms	Eastabuchie Mn	A	D
7.	Newberg Or	Newberg Or	A	D
8.	Arco Ga	Atco Ga	A	D
9.	Orocovis PR	Orocovls PR	A	D
10.	Bloomingburg Oh	Crampton Md	A	D
11.	Nashville Tn 37214	Nashville Tn 37214	A	D
12.	Charlson ND	Charlson ND	A	D
13.	Florence SC	Florence SD	A	D
14.	Burnett Mn	Barnett Mn	A	D
15.	Lakewood Wa	Lakewood Wa	A	D
16.	Moodus Ct	Moosup Ct	A	D
17.	Brighton NY 11200	Brighton NY 14600	A	D
18.	Akiak Ak	Aniak Ak	A	D
19.	Maskell Ne	Maskell Ne	A	D

KEY (CORRECT ANSWERS)

1.	D	11.	D
2.	A	12.	A
3.	A	13.	A
4.	A	14.	D
5.	D	15.	D
6.	D	16.	A
7.	A	17.	D
8.	D	18.	D
9.	A	19.	D
10.	D	20.	A

TEST 4

DIRECTIONS: This test is designed to measure your speed and accuracy. You are urged to work both quickly and accurately and to do correctly as many lists as you can in the time allowed. In this part, you will be given addresses to compare. If the two addresses are exactly <u>alike</u> in every way, circle the letter A. If the two addresses are <u>different</u> in any way, circle the letter D.

CIRCLE
CORRECT ANSWER

1.	Gaston SC	Gadsden SC	A	D
2.	Sonora Ca 95370	Sonora Ca 95310	A	D
3.	Glovergap WV	Clovergap WV	A	D
4.	Fairfax Al	Fairfield Al	A	D
5.	Cubero NM	Cubero NM	A	D
6.	Reedsville Wi	Reeseville Wi	A	D
7.	Ada Oh	Ava Oh	A	D
8.	Cheektowaga NY 14278	Cheektowaga NY 14278	A	D
9.	Cayuga NY	Cayuta NY	A	D
10.	Fruitland Id	Fruitland Id	A	D
11.	Cora WV	Cord WV	A	D
12.	Afton Tx	Anton Tx	A	D
13.	Hamptonville NC	Hamptonville NC	A	D
14.	Portola Ca 96100	Portola Ca 96100	A	D
15.	Sonoita Az	Sonoita Az	A	D
16.	Dunbarton NH 03300	Dunbarton NH 03300	A	D
17.	Benson Il	Benton Il	A	D
18.	Portland Or 97206	Portland Or 97206	A	D
19.	Flayton ND	Flaston ND	A	D
20.	Barnsdall Ok	Barnsdall Ok	A	D

KEY (CORRECT ANSWERS)

1. D
2. D
3. D
4. D
5. A

6. D
7. D
8. A
9. D
10. A

11. D
12. D
13. A
14. A
15. A

16. A
17. D
18. A
19. D
20. A

TEST 5

DIRECTIONS: This test is designed to measure your speed and accuracy. You are urged to work both quickly and accurately and to do correctly as many lists as you can in the time allowed. In this part, you will be given addresses to compare. If the two addresses are exactly <u>alike</u> in every way, circle the letter A. If the two addresses are <u>different</u> in any way, circle the letter D.

CIRCLE
CORRECT ANSWER

1.	Irmo SC	Irmo SC	A	D
2.	East Barnet Vt	East Barnet Vt	A	D
3.	Ellenburg Center NY 12900	Ellenburg Depot NY 12900	A	D
4.	Helena Mt	Helena Mt	A	D
5.	Grafton Wi	Granton Wi	A	D
6.	Columbia NC	Columbus NC	A	D
7.	Dumont Co	Dupont Co	A	D
8.	McClusky ND	McCloskey ND	A	D
9.	Sheldon SC	Shelton SC	A	D
10.	Fredericksburg Ia	Fredericksburg Ia	A	D
11.	Holden Vt	Holton Vt	A	D
12.	Kurlsruhe ND	Karlsruhe ND	A	D
13.	East Springfield Pa	West Springfield Pa	A	D
14.	Villa Prades PR	Villa Prades PR	A	D
15.	Cadmus Mi	Cadmus Mi	A	D
16.	New London NH 03200	New London NH 03200	A	D
17.	Anchorage Ak 95501	Anchorage Ak 99501	A	D
18.	Carciasville Tx 78547	Garciasville Tx 78547	A	D
19.	Edenton Oh	Edenton Oh	A	D
20.	Vernal Ut	Vernon Ut	A	D

KEY (CORRECT ANSWERS)

1.	A	11.	D
2.	A	12.	D
3.	D	13.	D
4.	A	14.	A
5.	D	15.	A
6.	D	16.	A
7.	D	17.	D
8.	D	18.	D
9.	D	19.	A
10.	A	20.	D

TEST 6

DIRECTIONS: This test is designed to measure your speed and accuracy. You are urged to work both quickly and accurately and to do correctly as many lists as you can in the time allowed. In this part, you will be given addresses to compare. If the two addresses are exactly <u>alike</u> in every way, circle the letter A. If the two addresses are <u>different</u> in any way, circle the letter D.

CIRCLE
CORRECT ANSWER

1. Tullahassee Ok   Tallahassee Ok   A   D
2. Carlton Wa   Carson Wa   A   D
3. Tucson Az 85721   Tucson Az 85751   A   D
4. Vermillion SD 57069   Vermillion SD 57069   A   D
5. Oxford NH   Orford NH   A   D
6. Evanston Wy   Evanston Wy   A   D
7. Gonzalez Fl 32560   Gonzalez Fl 32560   A   D
8. Clifton Tn   Clinton Tn   A   D
9. Lindsborg Ks   Lindsborg Ks   A   D
10. Greenbush Va   Greensbush Va   A   D
11. Paterson NJ 07400   Paterson NJ 07500   A   D
12. Monticello Mn   Monticello Mn   A   D
13. Haina Hi   Hana Hi   A   D
14. Barre Ma   Barre Ma   A   D
15. Beech Creek Ky 42300   Beech Grove Ky 42300   A   D
16. Biddeford Me 04005   Biddeford Me 04006   A   D
17. Richford NY   Richland NY   A   D
18. Shamko Or 97057   Shaneko Or 97057   A   D
19. Farmington NM   Framington NM   A   D
20. Goodwell Ok   Goodwell Ok   A   D

KEY (CORRECT ANSWERS

1. D
2. D
3. D
4. A
5. D

6. A
7. A
8. D
9. A
10. D

11. D
12. A
13. D
14. A
15. D

16. D
17. D
18. D
19. D
20. A

———

NAME AND NUMBER CHECKING
EXAMINATION SECTION
TEST 1

DIRECTIONS: This test is designed to measure your speed/and accuracy. You are urged to work both quickly and accurately and to do correctly as many lists as you can in the time allowed. The test consists of lists or pairs of names and numbers. Count the number of IDENTICAL pairs in each list. Then, select the correct number, 1, 2, 3, 4, 5, and indicate your choice in the space at the right. Two sample questions are presented for your guidance, together with the correct solutions.

SAMPLE LIST A
Adelphi College – Adelphia College
Braxton Corp – Braxeton Corp.
Wassaic State School – Wassaic State School
Central Islip State Hospital – Central Isllip State Hospital
Greenwich House – Greenwich House

NOTE: There are only two correct pairs—Wassaic State School and Greenwich House. Therefore, the CORRECT answer is 2.

SAMPLE LIST B
78453694 – 78453684
784530 – 784530
533 – 534
67845 – 67845
2368745 – 2368755

NOTE: There are only two correct pairs—784530 and 67845. Therefore, the CORRECT answer is 2.

LIST 1   1.____
     Diagnostic Clinic   – Diagnostic Clinic
     Yorkville Health   – Yorkville Health
     Meinhard Clinic   – Meinhart Clinic
     Corlears Clinic   – Carlears Clinic
     Tremont Diagnostic   – Tremont Diagnostic

LIST 2   2.____
     73526   – 73526
     7283627198   – 7283627198
     627   – 637
     728352617283   – 7283526178282
     6281   – 6281

2 (#1)

LIST 3   3.____
    Jefferson Clinic   – Jeffersen Clinic
    Mott Haven Center   – Mott Havan Center
    Bronx Hospital   – Bronx Hospital
    Montefiore Hospital   – Montifeore Hospital
    Beth Isreal Hospital   – Beth Israel Hospital

LIST 4   4.____
    936271826   – 936371826
    5271   – 5291
    82637192037   – 82637192037
    527182   – 5271882
    726354256   - 72635456

LIST 5   5.____
    Trinity Hospital   – Trinity Hospital
    Central Harlem   – Centrel Harlem
    St. Luke's Hospital   – St. Lukes' Hospital
    Mt. Sinai Hospital   – Mt. Sinia Hospital
    N.Y. Dispensery   – N.Y. Dispensary

LIST 6   6.____
    725361552637   – 725361555637
    7526378   – 7526377
    6975   – 6975
    82637481028   – 82637481028
    3427   – 3429

LIST 7   7.____
    Misericordia Hospital   – Miseracordia Hospital
    Lebonan Hospital   – Lebanon Hospital
    Gouverneur Hospital   – Gouverner Hospital
    German Polyclinic   – German Policlinic
    French Hospital   – French Hospital

LIST 8   8.____
    8277364933251   – 827364933351
    63728   – 63728
    367281   – 367281
    62733846273   – 6273846293
    62836   - 6283

LIST 9   9.____
    King's County Hospital   – Kings County Hospital
    St. Johns Long Island   – St. John's Long Island
    Bellevue Hospital   – Bellvue Hospital
    Beth David Hospital   – Beth David Hospital
    Samaritan Hospital   – Samariton Hospital

3 (#1)

LIST 10   10._____
   62836454   – 62836455
   42738267   – 42738369
   573829   – 573829
   738291627874   – 738291627874
   725   - 735

LIST 11   11._____
   Bloomingdal Clinic   – Bloomingdale Clinic
   Communitty Hospital   – Community Hospital
   Metroplitan Hospital   – Metropoliton Hospital
   Lenox Hill Hospital   – Lonex Hill Hospital
   Lincoln Hospital   – Lincoln Hospital

LIST 12   12._____
   6283364728   – 6283648
   627385   – 627383
   54283902   – 54283602
   63354   – 63354
   7283562781   - 7283562781

LIST 13   13._____
   Sydenham Hospital   – Sydanham Hospital
   Roosevalt Hospital   – Roosevelt Hospital
   Vanderbilt Clinic   – Vanderbild Clinic
   Women's Hospital   – Woman's Hospital
   Flushing Hospital   – Flushing Hospital

LIST 14   14._____
   62738   – 62738
   727355542321   – 72735542321
   263849332   – 263849332
   262837   – 263837
   47382912   - 47382922

LIST 15   15._____
   Episcopal Hospital   – Episcapal Hospital
   Flower Hospital   – Flouer Hospital
   Stuyvesent Clinic   – Stuyvesant Clinic
   Jamaica Clinic   – Jamaica Clinic
   Ridgwood Clinic   – Ridgewood Clinic

LIST 16   16._____
   628367299   – 628367399
   111   – 111
   118293304829   – 1182839489
   4448   – 4448
   333693678   - 333693678

4 (#1)

LIST 17   17.____
   Arietta Crane Farm   – Areitta Crane Farm
   Bikur Chilim Home   – Bikur Chilom Home
   Burke Foundation   – Burke Foundation
   Blythedale Home   – Blythdale Home
   Campbell Cottages   – Cambell Cottages

LIST 18   18.____
   32123   – 32132
   273893326783   – 27389326783
   473829   – 473829
   7382937   – 7383937
   3628890122332   - 36289012332

LIST 19   19.____
   Caraline Rest   – Caroline Rest
   Loreto Rest   – Loretto Rest
   Edgewater Creche   – Edgwater Creche
   Holiday Farm   – Holiday Farm
   House of St. Giles   – House of st. Giles

LIST 20   20.____
   557286777   – 55728677
   3678902   – 3678892
   1567839   – 1567839
   7865434712   – 7865344712
   9927382   - 9927382

LIST 21   21.____
   Isabella Home   – Isabela Home
   James A. Moore Home   – James A. More Home
   The Robin's Nest   – The Roben's Nest
   Pelham Home   – Pelam Home
   St. Eleanora's Home   – St. Eleanora's Home

LIST 22   22.____
   273648293048   – 273648293048
   334   – 334
   7362536478   – 7362536478
   7362819273   – 7362819273
   7362   - 7363

LIST 23   23.____
   St. Pheobe's Mission   – St. Phebe's Mission
   Seaside Home   – Seaside Home
   Speedwell Society   – Speedwell Society
   Valeria Home   – Valera Home
   Wiltwyck   - Wildwyck

5 (#1)

LIST 24
    63728   – 63738
    63728192736   – 63728192738
    428   – 458
    62738291527   – 62738291529
    63728192   - 63728192

24.____

LIST 25
    McGaffin   – McGafin
    David Ardslee   – David Ardslee
    Axton Supply   – Axeton Supply Co
    Alice Russell   – Alice Russell
    Dobson Mfg. Co.   – Dobsen Mfg. Co.

25.____

KEY (CORRECT ANSWERS)

1.	3		11.	1
2.	3		12.	2
3.	1		13.	1
4.	1		14.	2
5.	1		15.	1
6.	2		16.	3
7.	1		17.	1
8.	2		18.	1
9.	1		19.	1
10.	2		20.	2

21. 1
22. 4
23. 2
24. 1
25. 2

TEST 2

DIRECTIONS: This test is designed to measure your speed/and accuracy. You are urged to work both quickly and accurately and to do correctly as many lists as you can in the time allowed. The test consists of lists or pairs of names and numbers. Count the number of IDENTICAL pairs in each list. Then, select the correct number, 1, 2, 3, 4, 5, and indicate your choice in the space at the right.

LIST 1
    82637381028   – 82637281028
    928   – 928
    72937281028   – 72937281028
    7362   – 7362
    927382615   – 927382615

1.____

LIST 2
    Albee Theatre   – Albee Theatre
    Lapland Lumber Co.   – Laplund Lumber Co.
    Adelphi College   – Adelphi College
    Jones & Son Inc.   – Jones & Sons Inc.
    S.W. Ponds Co.   – S.W. Ponds Co.

2.____

LIST 3
    85345   – 85345
    895643278   – 895643277
    726352   – 726353
    632685   – 632685
    7263524   – 7236524

3.____

LIST 4
    Eagle Library   – Eagle Library
    Dodge Ltd.   – Dodge Co.
    Stromberg Carlson   – Stromberg Carlsen
    Clairice Ling   – Clairice Linng
    Mason Book Co.   – Matson Book Co.

4.____

LIST 5
    66273   – 66273
    629   – 629
    7382517283   – 7382517283
    637281   – 639281
    2738261   – 2788261

5.____

LIST 6
    Robert MacColl   – Robert McColl
    Buick Motor   – Buck Motors
    Murray Bay & Co. Ltd.   – Murray Bay Co. Ltd.
    L.T. Ltyle   – L.T. Lyttle
    A.S. Landas   – A.S. Landas

6.____

2 (#2)

LIST 7   7.____
    6271526374890   – 627152637490
    73526189   – 73526189
    5372   – 5392
    637281142   – 63728124
    4783946   – 4783046

LIST 8   8.____
    Tyndall Burke   – Tyndell Burke
    W. Briehl   – W. Briehl
    Burritt Publishing Co.   – Buritt Publishing Co.
    Frederick Breyer & Co.   – Frederick Breyer Co.
    Bailey Buulard   – Bailey Bullard

LIST 9   9.____
    634   – 634
    16837   – 163837
    273892223678   – 27389223678
    527182   – 527782
    3628901223   – 3629002223

LIST 10   10.____
    Ernest Boas   – Ernest Boas
    Rankin Barne   – Rankin Barnes
    Edward Appley   – Edward Appely
    Camel   – Camel
    Caiger Food Co.   – Caiger Food Co.

LIST 11   11.____
    6273   – 6273
    322   – 332
    15672839   – 15672839
    63728192637   – 63728192639
    738   – 738

LIST 12   12.____
    Wells Fargo Co.   – Wells Fargo Co.
    W.D. Brett   – W.D. Britt
    Tassco Co.   – Tassko Co.
    Republic Mills   – Republic Mill
    R.W. Burnham   – R.W. Burhnam

LIST 13   13.____
    7253529152   – 7283529152
    6283   – 6383
    52839102738   – 5283910238
    308   – 398
    82637201927   – 8263720127

LIST 14
    Schumacker Co.   – Shumacker Co.
    C.H. Caiger   – C.H. Caiger
    Abraham Strauss   – Abram Straus
    B.F. Boettjer   – B.F. Boettijer
    Cut-Rate Store   – Cut-Rate Stores

14.____

LIST 15
    15273826   – 15273826
    72537   – 73537
    726391027384   – 62639107384
    637389   – 627399
    725382910   – 725382910

15.____

LIST 16
    Hixby Ltd.   – Hixby Lt'd.
    S. Reiner   – S. Riener
    Reynard Co.   – Reynord Co.
    Esso Gassoline Co.   – Esso Gasolene Co.
    Belle Brock   – Belle Brock

16.____

LIST 17
    7245   – 7245
    819263728192   – 819263728172
    682537289   – 682537298
    789   – 789
    82936542891   – 82936542891

17.____

LIST 18
    Joseph Cartwright   – Joseph Cartwrite
    Foote Food Co.   – Foot Food Co.
    Weiman & Held   – Weiman & Held
    Sanderson Shoe Co.   – Sandersen Shoe Co.
    A.M. Byrne   – A.N. Byrne

18.____

LIST 19
    4738267   – 4738277
    63728   – 63729
    6283628901   – 6283628991
    918264   – 918264
    263728192037   – 2637728192073

19.____

LIST 20
    Exray Laboratories   – Exray Labratories
    Curley Toy Co.   – Curly Toy Co.
    J. Lauer & Cross   – J. Laeur & Cross
    Mireco Brands   – Mireco Brands
    Sandor Lorand   – Sandor Larand

20.____

4 (#2)

LIST 21   21._____
   607   – 609
   6405   – 6403
   976   – 996
   101267   – 101267
   2065432   – 20965432

LIST 22   22._____
   John Macy & Sons   – John Macy & Son
   Venus Pencil Co.   – Venus Pencil Co.
   Nell McGinnis   – Nell McGinnis
   McCutcheon & Co.   – McCutcheon & Co.
   Sun-Tan Oil   – Sun-Tan Oil

LIST 23   23._____
   703345700   – 703345700
   46754   – 466754
   3367490   – 3367490
   3379   – 3778
   47384   – 47394

LIST 24   24._____
   arthritis   – arthritis
   asthma   – asthma
   endocrine   – endocrene
   gastro-enterological – gastrol-enteralogical
   orthopedic   – orthopedic

LIST 25   25._____
   743829432   – 743828432
   998   – 998
   732816253902   – 732816252902
   46829   – 46830
   7439120249   – 7439210249

KEY (CORRECT ANSWERS)

1.	4	11.	3
2.	3	12.	1
3.	2	13.	1
4.	1	14.	1
5.	2	15.	2
6.	1	16.	1
7.	2	17.	3
8.	1	18.	1
9.	1	19.	1
10.	3	20.	1

21.	1
22.	4
23.	2
24.	3
25.	1

———

Memory for Addresses

DESCRIPTION OF THE TEST AND SAMPLE QUESTIONS

All Clerks in the Post Office have to learn a scheme during their training period. The Clerk uses the scheme to sort the mail to where it is going. He must have a good memory in order to learn the scheme. Carriers also need good memories.

In this test you will be given 25 addresses to remember. The addresses are divided into five groups. Each group of five addresses is in a box such as those below. Each box has a letter—A, B, C, D, or E. You will have to learn which letter goes with each address. You will be given time to study in the examination room. In order to practice for this test, you need to be timed.

While you are doing the practice test, find out what is the best way for you to memorize which letter goes with each address. Some people learn best by studying the addresses in one box; then covering it and seeing whether they can say the addresses to themselves. If they can say them, they then try to learn the next box. If they cannot, they study the names in the first box again; and then try to say the names with the box covered. They do this for all the boxes. Other people learn best by studying across the page. Still others do best by memorizing everything at once. If you do not know your best way, try different ways and see which one is best for you. Do not try to memorize the names by writing them down because you won't be allowed to write them in the official examination.

Hints for Memory for Addresses Test

- Be sure to spend the study period studying.
- Be sure to try to learn which letter goes with each address. It is to your advantage to learn as many as you can.
- Do not spend too much time on any one question.
- Do not get nervous about the time limit. (In the official test no one is expected to do all the questions in the time allowed.)
- If you are not sure of an answer, guess.

Sample Questions for Memory for Addresses

In this test you will have five boxes labeled A, B, C, D, and E. Each box contains five addresses. Three of the five are groups of street addresses like 1700–2599 Wood, 8500–8699 Lang, and 6200–6399 James, and two are names of places. They are different in each box.

You will also be given two lists of names. You will have to decide which box each name belongs in. When you are working on the first list, you will have the boxes with the names in front of you. When you are working on the second list, you will not be able to look at the boxes.

The addresses you will use for the Practice Test are given in the boxes below.

A	B	C	D	E
1700–2599 Wood Dushore 8500–8699 Lang Lott 6200–6399 James	2700–3299 Wood Jeriel 8700–9399 Lang Vanna 5700–6199 James	1300–1699 Wood Levering 9400–9499 Lang Ekron 6400–6499 James	3300–3599 Wood Bair 8000–8499 Lang Viborg 5000–5699 James	2600–2699 Wood Danby 9500–9999 Lang Lycan 4700–4999 James

Questions 1 through 5 show the way the questions look. You have to decide in which lettered box (A, B, C, D, or E) the address belongs and then mark that answer on the Sample Answer Sheet on this page.

1. Levering

    This address is in box C. So darken box C on the Sample Answer Sheet.

2. 2700–3299 Wood

    This address is in box B. So darken box B on the Sample Answer Sheet.

3. Vanna

    This address is in box B. So darken box B on the Sample Answer Sheet.

Now, you do questions 4 and 5.

4. 6200–6399 James

5. Bair

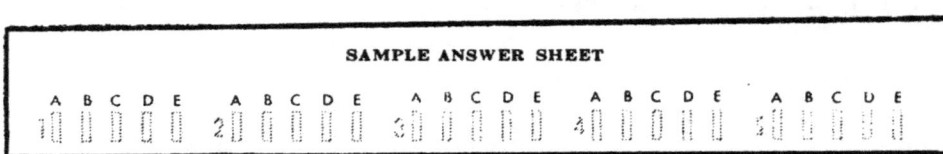

The answers for samples 4 and 5 are 4A and 5D.

Your practice test starts on the next page.

MEMORY FOR ADDRESSES—PRACTICE TEST
STUDY—*3 minutes*

Now turn back to page 2 and spend 3 minutes memorizing the addresses in the boxes. TRY TO LEARN THE LOCATION OF AS MANY ADDRESSES AS YOU CAN. Cover each box with your hand and see if you can repeat, to yourself, the addresses in that box.

When the 3 minutes for studying are up, turn to page 4 and continue with the practice.

List 1

WORK—*3 minutes*

For each question, mark the Sample Answer Sheet on the next page to show the letter of the box in which the address belongs. Try to remember the location of as many addresses as you can. If you are not sure of an address, guess. Work only 3 minutes.

A	B	C	D	E
1700–2599 Wood Dushore 8500–8699 Lang Lott 6200–6399 James	2700–3299 Wood Jeriel 8700–9399 Lang Vanna 5700–6199 James	1300–1699 Wood Levering 9400–9499 Lang Ekron 6400–6499 James	3300–3599 Wood Bair 8000–8499 Lang Viborg 5000–5699 James	2600–2699 Wood Danby 9500–9999 Lang Lycan 4700–4999 James

1. 6200–6399 James
2. 1700–2599 Wood
3. Bair
4. 1700–2599 Wood
5. Ekron
6. Viborg
7. Danby
8. 8500–8699 Lang

9. Lycan
10. 8000–8499 Lang
11. 4700–4999 James
12. 9400–9499 Lang
13. 2700–3299 Wood
14. Jeriel
15. 9500–9999 Lang
16. 1300–1699 Wood

17. 8700–9399 Lang
18. Levering
19. Vanna
20. 6400–6499 James
21. 3300–3599 Wood
22. Dushore
23. Lycan
24. 5700–6199 James

25. Lott
26. Viborg
27. Jeriel
28. 5000–5699 James
29. 2600–2699 Wood
30. 4700–4999 James
31. 2700–3299 Wood
32. 8000–8499 Lang

33. Ekron
34. 3300–3599 Wood
35. 9400–9499 Lang
36. 6200–6399 James
37. 2600–2699 Wood
38. 8500–8699 Lang
39. Levering
40. Lott

41. Bair
42. 1700–2599 Wood
43. 6400–6499 James
44. 9500–9999 Lang
45. Jeriel
46. 4700–4999 James
47. Dushore
48. Lycan

49. 1700–2599 Wood
50. 6200–6399 James
51. Vanna
52. Ekron
53. 8700–9399 Lang
54. Bair
55. 2600–2699 Wood
56. Dushore

57. 5700–6199 James
58. 1300–1699 Wood
59. Levering
60. Lott
61. Jeriel
62. 2600–2699 Wood
63. Lott
64. 4700–4999 James

65. Dushore
66. Danby
67. 8500–8699 Lang
68. Vanna
69. 2700–3299 Wood
70. 9500–9999 Lang
71. Viborg
72. Ekron

73. 6200–6399 James
74. 2600–2699 Wood
75. Levering
76. Lott
77. 1300–1699 Wood
78. Bair
79. Lycan
80. 5700–6199 James

81. Levering
82. 8700–9399 Lang
83. 5000–5699 James
84. 1700–2599 Wood
85. Jeriel
86. 6200–6399 James
87. Ekron
88. 2700–3299 Wood

STOP.

If you finish before the 3 minutes are up, go back and check your answers for the questions on this page for the rest of the 3 minutes.

When the 3 minutes are up, go on to page 6.

SAMPLE ANSWER SHEET

List 2

WORK—*3 minutes*

Now do these questions without looking back at the boxes with the addresses in them.

For each question, mark your answer on the Sample Answer Sheet on the next page. If you are not sure of an answer, guess.

1. Jeriel
2. Dushore
3. 5000–5699 James
4. 1300–1699 Wood
5. 8500–8699 Lang
6. Bair
7. 5700–6199 James
8. Levering

9. Danby
10. Viborg
11. 8000–8499 Lang
12. 2700–3299 Wood
13. 9400–9499 Lang
14. 3300–3599 Wood
15. 4700–4999 James
16. 9500–9999 Lang

17. Ekron
18. 1300–1699 Wood
19. Vanna
20. Lycan
21. 8700–9399 Lang
22. Dushore
23. 6200–6399 James
24. Lott

25. 2700–3299 Wood
26. 5700–6199 James
27. Levering
28. 9500–9999 Lang
29. 2600–2699 Wood
30. 3300–3599 Wood
31. Viborg
32. 9400–9499 Lang

33. Jeriel
34. Bair
35. 8500–8699 Lang
36. 1700–2599 Wood
37. 8000–8499 Lang
38. Danby
39. Ekron
40. 4700–4999 James

41. Dushore
42. Vanna
43. 5000–5699 James
44. Lott
45. 1300–1699 Wood
46. Levering
47. 5700–6199 James
48. 9500–9999 Lang

49. Bair
50. 8700–9399 Lang
51. 6200–6399 James
52. 9400–9499 Lang
53. Viborg
54. 8000–8499 Lang
55. 4700–4999 James
56. Lycan

57. Vanna
58. Danby
59. 5700–6199 James
60. Lott
61. 2700–3299 Wood
62. 5000–5699 James
63. 1700–2599 Wood
64. 8000–8499 Lang

65. 9400–9499 Lang
66. Jeriel
67. 9500–9999 Lang
68. Dushore
69. 2600–2699 Wood
70. 8500–8699 Lang
71. Levering
72. 5000–5699 James

73. Dushore
74. 8000–8499 Lang
75. Bair
76. Ekron
77. 6200–6399 James
78. 3300–3599 Wood
79. 8700–9399 Lang
80. Viborg

81. 4700–4999 James
82. Lycan
83. 1700–2599 Wood
84. 8500–8699 Lang
85. 1300–1699 Wood
86. Jeriel
87. Danby
88. 6400–6499 James

STOP.

If you finish before the end of 3 minutes, go back and be sure that you are satisfied with your answers.

Second Study

STUDY—*5 minutes*

You can see that memory is important in this test.

Now turn back to page 2 and spend 5 minutes memorizing the addresses in the boxes. TRY TO MEMORIZE THE LOCATION OF AS MANY ADDRESSES AS YOU CAN. Cover each box with your hand and see if you can repeat, to yourself, the addresses in that box.

When the 5 minutes for studying are up, turn to page 8 and continue with the practice.

SAMPLE ANSWER SHEET

List 1—Second Time

WORK—*5 minutes*

For each question, mark your answer on the Sample Answer Sheet on the next page. Try to remember the location of as many addresses as you can.

A	B	C	D	E
1700–2599 Wood Dushore 8500–8699 Lang Lott 6200–6399 James	2700–3299 Wood Jeriel 8700–9399 Lang Vanna 5700–6199 James	1300–1699 Wood Levering 9400–9499 Lang Ekron 6400–6499 James	3300–3599 Wood Bair 8000–8499 Lang Viborg 5000–5699 James	2600–2699 Wood Danby 9500–9999 Lang Lycan 4700–4999 James

1. 6200–6399 James
2. 1700–2599 Wood
3. Bair
4. 1700–2599 Wood
5. Ekron
6. Viborg
7. Danby
8. 8500–8699 Lang
9. Lycan
10. 8000–8499 Lang
11. 4700–4999 James
12. 9400–9499 Lang
13. 2700–3299 Wood
14. Jeriel
15. 9500–9999 Lang
16. 1300–1699 Wood
17. 8700–9399 Lang
18. Levering
19. Vanna
20. 6400–6499 James
21. 3300–3599 Wood
22. Dushore
23. Lycan
24. 5700–6199 James
25. Lott
26. Viborg
27. Jeriel
28. 5000–5699 James
29. 2600–2699 Wood
30. 4700–4999 James
31. 2700–3299 Wood
32. 8000–8499 Lang
33. Ekron
34. 3300–3599 Wood
35. 9400–9499 Lang
36. 6200–6399 James
37. 2600–2699 Wood
38. 8500–8699 Lang
39. Levering
40. Lott
41. Bair
42. 1700–2599 Wood
43. 6400–6499 James
44. 9500–9999 Lang
45. Jeriel
46. 4700–4999 James
47. Dushore
48. Lycan
49. 1700–2599 Wood
50. 6200–6399 James
51. Vanna
52. Ekron
53. 8700–9399 Lang
54. Bair
55. 2600–2699 Wood
56. Dushore
57. 5700–6199 James
58. 1300–1699 Wood
59. Levering
60. Lott
61. Jeriel
62. 2600–2699 Wood
63. Lott
64. 4700–4999 James
65. Dushore
66. Danby
67. 8500–8699 Lang
68. Vanna
69. 2700–3299 Wood
70. 9500–9999 Lang
71. Viborg
72. Ekron
73. 6200–6399 James
74. 2600–2699 Wood
75. Levering
76. Lott
77. 1300–1699 Wood
78. Bair
79. Lycan
80. 5700–6199 James
81. Levering
82. 8700–9399 Lang
83. 5000–5699 James
84. 1700–2599 Wood
85. Jeriel
86. 6200–6399 James
87. Ekron
88. 2700–3299 Wood

STOP.

If you finish before the 5 minutes are up, go back and check your answers for the questions on this page.

At the end of 5 minutes, turn to page 10.

SAMPLE ANSWER SHEET

List 2—Second Time

WORK—*5 minutes*

This is the section that counts. The other times were to help you learn the addresses.

Do these questions without looking back at the boxes with the addresses in them. Work for 5 minutes.

For each question, mark the Sample Answer Sheet on the next page to show the letter of the box in which the address belongs.

1. Jeriel
2. Dushore
3. 5000–5699 James
4. 1300–1699 Wood
5. 8500–8699 Lang
6. Bair
7. 5700–6199 James
8. Levering

9. Danby
10. Viborg
11. 8000–8499 Lang
12. 2700–3299 Wood
13. 9400–9499 Lang
14. 3300–3599 Wood
15. 4700–4999 James
16. 9500–9999 Lang

17. Ekron
18. 1300–1699 Wood
19. Vanna
20. Lycan
21. 8700–9399 Lang
22. Dushore
23. 6200–6399 James
24. Lott

25. 2700–3299 Wood
26. 5700–6199 James
27. Levering
28. 9500–9999 Lang
29. 2600–2699 Wood
30. 3300–3599 Wood
31. Viborg
32. 9400–9499 Lang

33. Jeriel
34. Bair
35. 8500–8699 Lang
36. 1700–2599 Wood
37. 8000–8499 Lang
38. Danby
39. Ekron
40. 4700–4999 James

41. Dushore
42. Vanna
43. 5000–5699 James
44. Lott
45. 1300–1699 Wood
46. Levering
47. 5700–6199 James
48. 9500–9999 Lang

49. Bair
50. 8700–9399 Lang
51. 6200–6399 James
52. 9400–9499 Lang
53. Viborg
54. 8000–8499 Lang
55. 4700–4999 James
56. Lycan

57. Vanna
58. Danby
59. 5700–6199 James
60. Lott
61. 2700–3299 Wood
62. 5000–5699 James
63. 1700–2599 Wood
64. 8000–8499 Lang

65. 9400–9499 Lang
66. Jeriel
67. 9500–9999 Lang
68. Dushore
69. 2600–2699 Wood
70. 8500–8699 Lang
71. Levering
72. 5000–5699 James

73. Dushore
74. 8000–8499 Lang
75. Bair
76. Ekron
77. 6200–6399 James
78. 3300–3599 Wood
79. 8700–9399 Lang
80. Viborg

81. 4700–4999 James
82. Lycan
83. 1700–2599 Wood
84. 8500–8699 Lang
85. 1300–1699 Wood
86. Jeriel
87. Danby
88. 6400–6499 James

STOP.

If you finish before the 5 minutes are up, go back and check your answers.

At the end of the 5 minutes, compare your answers with those given in the Correct Answers for sample questions on page 11.

SAMPLE ANSWER SHEET

PART B

Now check your answers by comparing your answers with the correct answers shown below.

CORRECT ANSWERS

PART B

Count how many you got right, and write that number on this line ⟶ Number Right ____

Now count how many you got wrong, and write that number on this line ⟶ Number Wrong ____

Divide the Number Wrong by 4, and write the answer on this line ⟶ ¼ Number Wrong ____

Subtract the ¼ Number Wrong from the Number Right, and write the Difference on this line ⟶ Total Score ____

(The meaning of your Test Score will be found on page 12.)

Meaning of Test Score

If your Total Score is *44 or more*, you have a Good score.

If your Total Score is from *26 to 43*, you have a Fair score.

If your Total Score is *25 or less*, you are not doing too well.

You may be going too slowly, or you may be making too many mistakes. You need more practice.

Following Oral Directions

DESCRIPTION OF THE TEST AND SAMPLE QUESTIONS

Since it is important that each employee does exactly as he is instructed, this test is used to make sure that each applicant can and will listen carefully and follow through without extra supervision.

The directions in the test are not hard to follow, but you must listen carefully and do exactly what you are told to do.

In order to do this practice section, you must have a friend who will read the directions to you. *Hints for Doing the Test of Following Oral Directions*
- Listen carefully to the directions.
- Do exactly what the examiner tells you to do.
- Do not try to get ahead of the examiner.
- If you missed an instruction, wait for the next one.
- Make sure that you darken only one box for each number on the answer sheet.

The material which yon will use for practice on the Following Oral Directions Test is on pages 2-8.

Do not read the material on pages 9-13 yourself; because, if you do, you will lose the value of this practice.

Following Oral Directions-Sample Questions

The directions are to be read at the rate of 80 words per minute. Since not everybody speaks at this speed, your friend should practice reading the 1-minute practice on page 9 until he can read it in exactly 1 minute whenever he wants to. He will also need a watch with a second hand.

To do the sample questions tear out page 9 which has the 1-minute practice and the directions for the sample questions. Give it to your friend to use. (Each friend who is helping you will have to use it to practice, so don't throw it away.)

When your friend reads the directions to you, listen carefully and do what he says. If you fall behind and miss a direction, don't get excited. Let that one go and listen for the next one. Since B and D sound very much alike, he will say "B as in baker" when he means B and "D as in dog" when he means D.

He will tell you some things to do with the 5 sample questions below. Then, when he tells you to darken a box on the Sample Answer Sheet, use the one on this page.

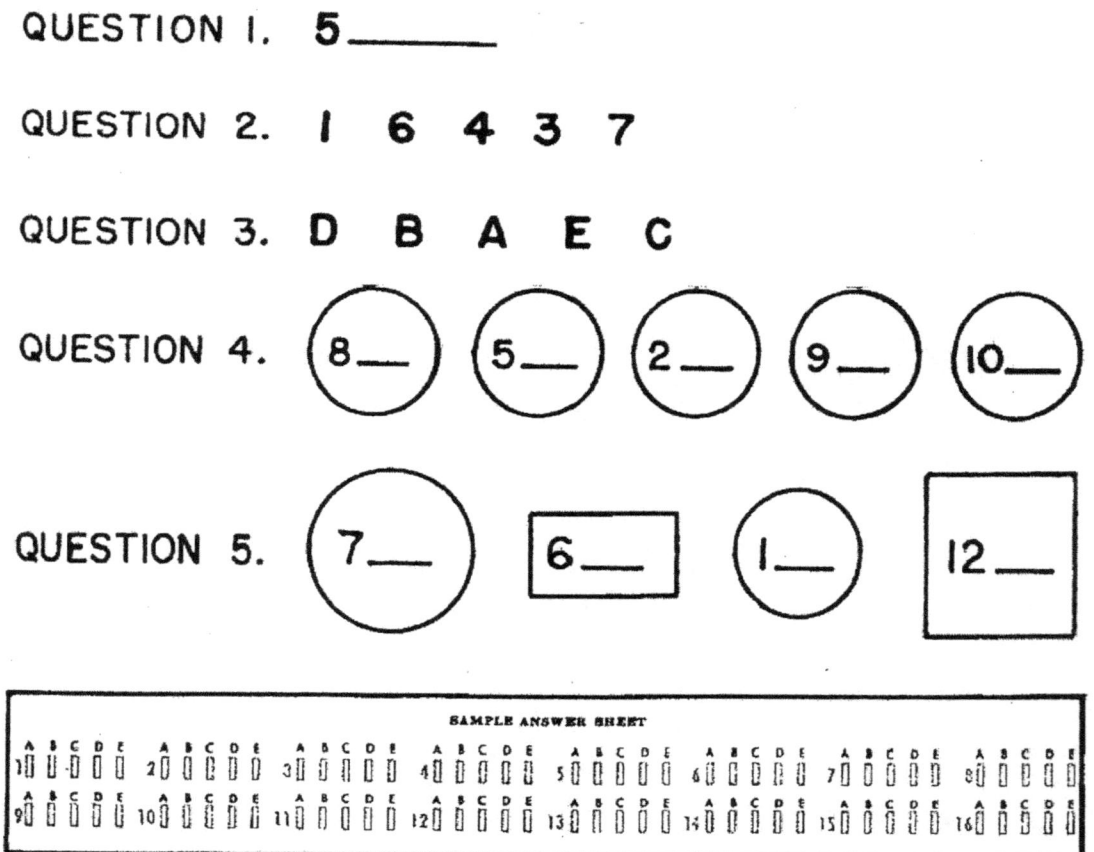

WORKSHEET FOR PRACTICE TEST 1

1. 45____   43____   83____

2. |__A| |__E| |__C| |__B| |__D|

3. 69 87 50 54 25 47 20 80 27

4. (71__) (36__) (49__) (11__)

5. [42__] (44__) (14__) [56__]

6. (88__) (68__) (61__) (70__) (34__)

7. 28   67   29   77   26

8. | A | B | C |
   | CHESTNUT STREET | HYDE PARK | PRUDENTIAL PLAZA |
   | ____ | ____ | ____ |

9. [85__] [86__] [63__] [39__]

Now check your answers by comparing your answers with the correct answers shown below.

Your Test Score on this Practice Test is the number you got right.

Count how many you got right, and write that number on this line ⟶ _____

Meaning of Test Score

If your Test Score is *15 or 16*, you have a Good score.

If your Test Score is *13 or 14*, you have a Fair score.

If your Test Score is *12 or less*, you are not doing too well.

You may be working too slowly or you may not be doing exactly what you are told to do.

You need more practice.

WORKSHEET FOR PRACTICE TEST 2

1. 40 85 17 87 52 55 56 45 75

2. | 65 __ | | 37 __ | | 12 __ | | 4 __ |

3. X O O O X O O X X O X O X

4. | 78 __ | (25 __) | 27 __ | (73 __)

5. 88   2   69   84   34

6. (63 __) (38 __) (76 __) (53 __) (57 __)

7. | 435 __ B | | 466 __ C | | 474 __ E | | 467 __ A | | 489 __ D |

8. 79 _____   39 _____

9. | __ C | | __ E | | __ A | | __ D | | __ B |

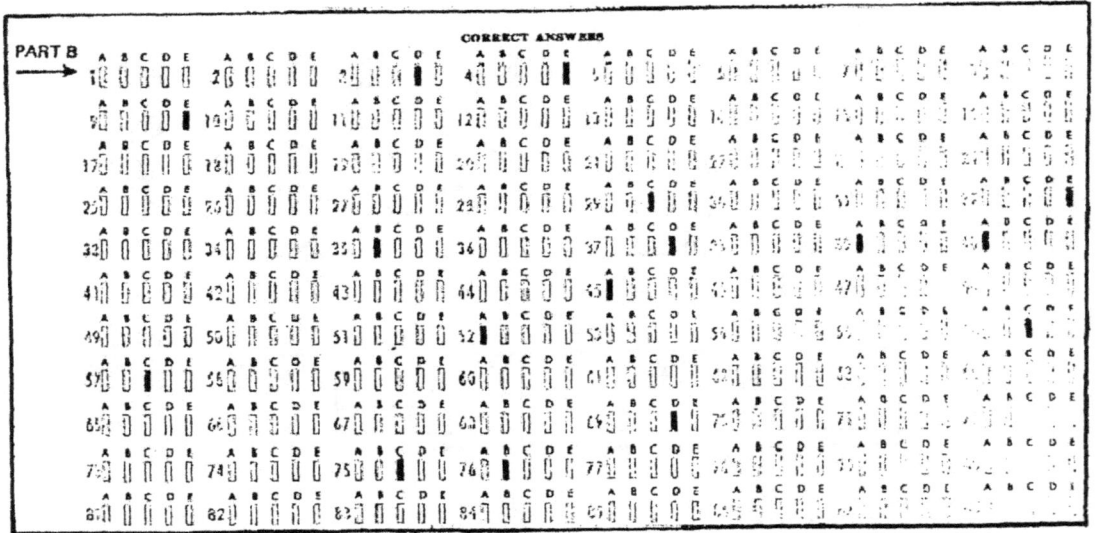

Now check your answers by comparing your answers with the correct answers shown below.

Your Test Score on this Practice Test is the number you got right.

    Count how many you got right, and write that number on this line ———————→ _____

Meaning of Test Score

    If your Test Score *is 15 or 16,* you have a Good score.

    If your Test Score is *13 or 14,* you have a Fair score.

    If your Test Score is *12 or less,* you are not doing too well.

      You may be working too slowly or you may not be doing exactly what you are told to do.

        You need more practice.

WORKSHEET FOR PRACTICE TEST 3

1.   59   35   62   58   8

2. (__C)   (__A)   (__D)   (__E)   (__B)

3.   15 _____   20 _____

4. [3__]   [37__]   [36__]   CURE   DAMP   BEAR

5.   A   C   B   A   B   D   C   E   D

6. [48__]   [28__]   [22__]   [43__]

7.   51 _____   69 _____   50 _____

8. (65__)   (13__)   (87__)   (31__)   (17__)

9. [55__]   [44__]   [74__]   [25__]

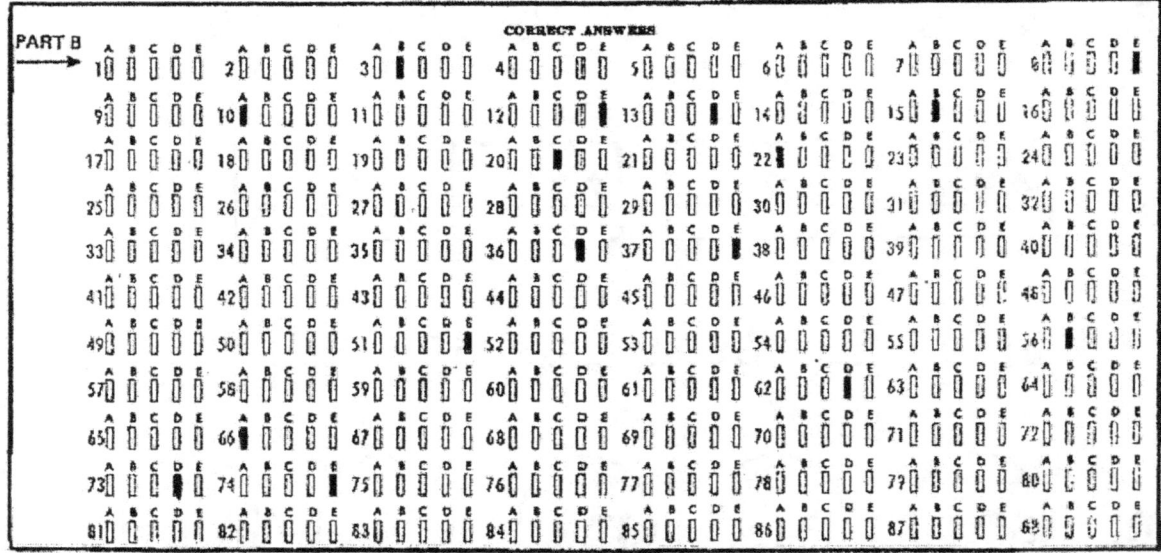

Now check your answers by comparing your answers with the correct answers shown below.

Your Test Score on this Practice Test is the number you got right.

Count how many you got right, and write that number on this line ⟶ _____

Meaning of Test Score

If your Test Score is *15 or 16,* you have a Good score.

If your Test Spore is *13 or 14,* you have a Fair score.

If your Test Score is *12 or less,* you are not doing too well.

You may be working too slowly or you may not be doing exactly what you are told to do.

You need more practice.

For The Person Who Will Read The Following Oral Directions Test to You

The directions should be read at about 80 words per minute. Practice reading aloud the material in the box below until you can do it in exactly 1 minute. This will give you a feel for the way you should read the test material.

1-MINUTE PRACTICE
(This is for practice in reading aloud. It is not the sample test.)

> Look at line 20 in your work booklet. There are two circles and two boxes of different sizes with numbers in them. If 7 is less than 3 and if 2 is smaller than 4, write a G in the larger circle. Otherwise write B as in baker in the smaller box. Now on your Code Sheet darken the space for the number-letter combination in the box or circle.

DIRECTIONS: (The words in parentheses should *not* be read aloud. They tell you how long you should pause at the various spots. You should time the pauses with a watch with a second hand. The instruction "Pause slightly" means that you should stop long enough to take a breath.) You should not repeat any directions.

THIS IS THE SAMPLE.

> You are to follow the instructions that I read to you. I cannot repeat them.
>
> Look at the Sample Questions. Question 1 has a number and a line beside it. On the line write an A. (Pause 2 seconds.) Now on the Sample Answer Sheet, find number 5 (pause 2 seconds) and darken the box for the letter you just wrote on the line. (Pause 5 seconds.)
>
> Look at Question 2. (Pause slightly.) Draw a line under the third number. (Pause 2 seconds.) Now on the Sample Answer Sheet, find the number under which you just drew a line and darken box B as in baker for that number. (Pause 5 seconds.)
>
> Look at the letters in Question 3. (Pause slightly.) Draw a line under the third letter in the line. (Pause 2 seconds.) Now on your answer sheet, find number 9 (pause 2 seconds) and darken the box for the letter under which you drew a line. (Pause 5 seconds.)
>
> Look at the five circles in Question 4. (Pause slightly.) Each circle has a number and a line in it. Write D as in dog on the blank in the last circle. (Pause 2 seconds.) Now on the Sample Answer Sheet, darken the space for the number-letter combination that is in the circle you just wrote in. (Pause 5 seconds.)
>
> Look at Question 5. (Pause slightly.) There are two circles and two boxes of different sizes with numbers in them. (Pause slightly.) If 4 is more than 2 and if 5 is less than 3, write A in the smaller circle. (Pause slightly.) Otherwise write C in the larger box. (Pause 2 seconds.) Now on the Sample Answer Sheet, darken the space for the number-letter combination in the box or circle in which you just wrote. (Pause 5 seconds.)
>
> Now look at the Sample Answer Sheet. (Pause slightly.) You should have darkened spaces 4B, 5A, 9A, 10D, and 12C on the Sample Answer Sheet.

FOLLOWING ORAL DIRECTIONS-PRACTICE TEST 1

When you are ready to try Practice Test 1, tear this sheet out and give it to your friend who is helping you practice the Following Oral Directions Test.

To the Person Who Is to Read the Directions Directions are to be read at the rate of 80 words per minute. Do not read aloud the material which is in parentheses. Do not repeat any directions.

Read the following directions aloud.

For this practice test you are to use the worksheet that is on page 3 and the answer sheet which is on page 4 . (Pause until the person studying has turned to page 3)

Look at line 1 on your worksheet. (Pause slightly.) Next to the left-hand number write the letter E. (Pause 2 seconds.) Now on your answer sheet, find the space for the number beside which you wrote and darken box E. (Pause 5 seconds.)

Now look at line 2 on your worksheet. (Pause slightly.) There are 5 boxes. Each box has a letter. (Pause slightly.) In the fifth box write the answer to this question: Which of the following numbers is largest: 18, 9, 15, 19, 13? (Pause 5 seconds.) Now on your answer sheet, darken the space for the number-letter combination that is in the box you just wrote in. (Pause 5 seconds.) In the fourth box on the same line do nothing. In the third box write 5. (Pause 2'seconds.) Now on your answer sheet, darken the space for the number-letter combination that is in the box you just wrote in. (Pause 5 seconds.) In the second box, write the answer to this question: How many hours are there in a day? (Pause 2 seconds.) Now on your answer sheet, darken the space for the number-letter combination that is in the box you just wrote in. (Pause 5 seconds.)

Look at line 3 on your worksheet. (Pause slightly.) Draw a line under every number that is more than 50 but less than 85. (Pause 12 seconds.) Now on your answer sheet, for each number that you drew a line under, darken box D as in dog. (Pause 25 seconds.)

Look at line 4 on your worksheet. (Pause slightly.) Write a B as in baker in the third circle. (Pause 2 seconds.) Now on your answer sheet, find the number in that circle and darken box B for that number. (Pause 5 seconds.)

Look at line 4 again. (Pause slightly.) Write C in the first circle. (Pause 2 seconds.) Now on your answer sheet, find the number in that circle and darken box C for that number. (Pause 5 seconds.)

Look at line 5 on your worksheet. (Pause slightly.) There are two circles and two boxes of different sizes with numbers in them. (Pause slightly.) If 4 is more than 6 and if 9 is less than 7, write D as in dog in the smaller box. (Pause slightly.) Otherwise write A in the larger circle. (Pause 2 seconds.) Now on your answer sheet, darken the space for the number-letter combination for the box or circle you just wrote in. (Pause 5 seconds.)

Now look at line 6 on your worksheet. (Pause slightly.) Write an E in the second circle. (Pause 2 seconds.) Now on your answer sheet, find the number in that circle and darken box E for that number. (Pause 5 seconds.)

Now look at line 6 again. (Pause slightly.) Write a B as in baker in the middle circle. (Pause 2 seconds.) Now on your answer sheet, find the number in that circle and darken box B as in baker for that number. (Pause 5 seconds.)

Look at the numbers on line 7 on your worksheet. (Pause slightly.) Draw a line under the largest number in the line. (Pause 2 seconds.) Now on your answer sheet, find the space for that number and darken box C for that number. (Pause 5 seconds.)

Now look at line 7 again. (Pause slightly.) Draw a circle around the smallest number in the line. (Pause 2 seconds.) Now on your answer sheet, find the space for the number which you just drew a circle around and darken box A for that number. (Pause 5 seconds.)

(over)

Now look at line 8 on your worksheet. There are 3 boxes with words and letters in them. (Pause slightly.) Each box represents a station in a large city. Station A delivers mail in the Chestnut Street area, Station B delivers mail in Hyde Park, and Station C delivers mail in the Prudential Plaza. Mr. Adams lives in Hyde Park. Write the number 30 on the line inside the box which represents the station that delivers Mr. Adams' mail. (Pause 2 seconds.) Now on your answer sheet, find the space for number 30 and darken the box for the letter that is in the box you just wrote in. (Pause 5 seconds.)

Now look at line 9 on your worksheet. (Pause slightly.) Write a D as in dog in the second box. (Pause 2 seconds.) Now on your answer sheet, find the number that is in the box you just wrote in and darken box D as in dog for that number. (Pause 5 seconds.)

Now check your answers by comparing them with the correct answers on page 4.

FOLLOWING ORAL DIRECTIONS-PRACTICE TEST 2

When you are ready to try Practice Test 2, tear this sheet out and give it to your friend who is helping you practice the Following Oral Directions Test.

To the Person Who Is to Read the Directions The Directions are to be read at the rate of 80 words per minute. Do not read aloud the material which is in parentheses. Do not repeat any directions.

Read the following directions aloud.

For this practice test you are to use the worksheet that is on page 26 and the answer sheet which is on page 6 . (Pause until the person studying has turned to page 5 .)

Look at line 1 on your worksheet. (Pause slightly.) Draw a line under every number that is more than 35 but less than 55. (Pause 12 seconds.) Now on your answer sheet, for each number that you drew a line under darken box A. (Pause 25 seconds.)

Now look at line 1 on your worksheet again. (Pause slightly.) Draw two lines under every number that is more than 55 and less than 80. (Pause 12 seconds.) Now on your answer sheet for each number that you drew two lines under darken box C. (Pause 25 seconds.)

Look at line 2 on your worksheet. (Pause slightly.) Write an E in the last box. (Pause 2 seconds.) Now on your answer sheet, find the number in that box and darken box E for that number. (Pause 5 seconds.)

Now look at line 2 on your worksheet again. (Pause slightly.) Write a D as in dog in the second box. (Pause 2 seconds.) Now on your answer sheet, find the number in that box and darken box D as in dog for that number. (Pause 5 seconds.)

Look at line 3 on your worksheet. (Pause slightly.) Draw a line under every "X" in the line. (Pause 5 seconds.) Count the number of lines that you have drawn, add 3, and write that number at the end of the line. (Pause 5 seconds.) Now on your answer sheet, find that number and darken space E for that number. (Pause 5 seconds.)

Look at line 4 on your worksheet. (Pause slightly.) If the number in the right-hand box is larger than the number in the left-hand circle, add 4 to the number in the left-hand circle, and change the number in the circle to this number. (Pause 8 seconds.) Then write C next to the new number. (Pause slightly.) Otherwise, write A next to the number in the smaller box. (Pause 3 seconds.) Now on your answer sheet, darken the space for the number-letter combination that is in the box or circle you just wrote in. (Pause 5 seconds.)

Now look at line 5 on your worksheet. (Pause slightly.) Draw a line under the middle number in the line. (Pause 2 seconds.) Now on your answer sheet, find the number under which you just drew the line and darken box D as in dog for that number. (Pause 5 seconds.)

Now look at line 6 on your worksheet. (Pause slightly.) Write a B as in baker in the third circle. (Pause 2 seconds.) Now on your answer sheet, find the number in that circle and darken box B as in baker for that number. (Pause 5 seconds.)

Now look at line 6 again. (Pause slightly.) Write a C in the last circle. (Pause 2 seconds.) Now on your answer sheet, find the number in that circle and darken box C for that number. (Pause 5 seconds.)

Look at the drawings on line 7 on your worksheet. The number in each box is the number of employees in a post office. (Pause slightly.) In the box for the post office with the smallest number of employees, write on the line the last two figures of the number of employees. (Pause 5 seconds.) Now on your answer sheet, darken the space for the number-letter combination that is in the box you just wrote in. (Pause 5 seconds.)

Now look at line 8 on your worksheet. (Pause slightly.) Write an A on the line next to the right-hand number. (Pause 2 seconds.) Now on your answer sheet find the space for the number next to which you just wrote and darken box A. (Pause 5 seconds.)

Look at line 9 on your worksheet. (Pause slightly.) In the fourth box, write the answer to this question: How many feet are in a yard? (Pause 2 seconds.) Now on your answer sheet darken the space for the number-letter combination that is in the box you just wrote in. (Pause 5 seconds.)

Look at line 9 again. (Pause slightly.) In the second box, write the number 32, (Pause 2 seconds.) Now on your answer sheet, find the number-letter combination that is in the box you just wrote in. (Pause 5 seconds.)

Now check your answers by comparing them with the Correct Answers on page 6.

FOLLOWING ORAL DIRECTIONS–PRACTICE TEST 3

When you are ready to try Practice Test 3, tear this sheet out and give it to your friend who is helping you practice the Following Oral Directions Test.

To the Person Who Is to Read the Directions–The Directions are to be read at the rate of 80 words per minute. Do not read the material which is in parentheses aloud. Do not repeat any directions.

Read the following directions aloud.

For this practice test you are to use the worksheet that is on page 28 and the answer sheet that is on page 29. (Pause until the person preparing for the examination has turned to page 28.)

Look at line 1 on your worksheet. (Pause slightly.) Draw a line under the largest number in the line. (Pause 2 seconds.) Now on your answer sheet, find the number under which you just drew a line and darken box D as in dog for that number. (Pause 5 seconds.)

Look at line 1 on your worksheet again. (Pause slightly.) Draw two lines under the smallest number in the line. (Pause 2 seconds.) Now on your answer sheet, find the number under which you just drew two lines and darken box E. (Pause 5 seconds.)

Look at the circles in line 2 on your worksheet. (Pause slightly.) In the second circle, write the answer to this question: How much is 6 plus 4? (Pause 8 seconds.) In the third circle, write the answer to this question: Which of the following numbers is largest: 67, 48, 15, 73, 61? (Pause 5 seconds.) In the fourth circle, write the answer to this question: How many months are there in a year? (Pause 2 seconds.) Now, on your answer sheet, darken the number-letter combinations that are in the circles you wrote in. (Pause 10 seconds.)

Now look at line 3 on your worksheet. (Pause slightly.) Write the letter C on the blank next to the right-hand number. (Pause 2 seconds.) Now on your answer sheet, find the space for the number beside which you wrote and darken box C. (Pause 5 seconds.)

Now look at line 3 on your worksheet again. (Pause slightly.) Write the letter B as in baker on the blank next to the left-hand number. (Pause 2 seconds.) Now on your answer sheet, find the space for the number beside which you just wrote and darken box B as in baker. (Pause 5 seconds.)

Look at the boxes and words in line 4 on your worksheet. (Pause slightly.) Write the first letter of the second word in the third box. (Pause 2 seconds.) Write the last letter of the first word in the second box. (Pause 2 seconds.) Write the first letter of the third word in the first box. (Pause 2 seconds.) Now on your answer sheet, darken the spaces for the number-letter combinations that are in the three boxes you just wrote in. (Pause 10 seconds.)

Look at the letters on line 5 on your worksheet. (Pause slightly.) Draw a line under the fifth letter in the line. (Pause 2 seconds.) Now on your answer sheet, find the number 56 (pause 2 seconds) and darken the space for the letter under which you drew a line. (Pause 5 seconds.)

Look at the letters on line 5 on your worksheet again. (Pause slightly.) Draw two lines under the fourth letter in the line. (Pause 2 seconds.) Now on your answer sheet, find the number 66 (pause 2 seconds) and darken the space for the letter under which you drew two lines. (Pause 5 seconds.)

Look at the drawings on line 6 on your worksheet. (Pause slightly.) The four boxes indicate the number of buildings in four different carrier routes. In the box for the route with the fewest number of buildings, write an A. (Pause 2 seconds.) Now on your answer sheet, darken the space for the number-letter combination that is in the box you just wrote in. (Pause 5 seconds.)

Now look at line 7 on your worksheet. (Pause slightly.) If fall comes before summer, write the letter B as in baker on the line next to the middle number. (Pause slightly.) Otherwise, write an E on the blank next to the left-hand number. (Pause 5 seconds.) Now on your answer sheet, darken the space for the number-letter combination that you hare just written. (Pause 5 seconds.)

Now look at line 8 on your worksheet. (Pause slightly.) Write a D as in dog in the circle with the lowest number. (Pause 2 seconds.) Now on your answer sheet, darken the space for the number-letter combination that is in the circle you just wrote in. (Pause 5 seconds.)

Look at the drawings in line 9 on your worksheet. The four boxes are planes for carrying mail. (Pause slightly.) The plane with the highest number is to be loaded first. Write an E in the box with the highest number. (Pause 2 seconds.) Now on your answer sheet, darken the space for the number-letter combination that is in the box you just wrote in. (Pause 5 seconds.)

Now check your answers by comparing them with the Correct Answers on page 8.

FOLLOWING ORAL DIRECTIONS

COMMENTARY

A large part of any job is listening to the supervisor and following his instructions. Since it is important that each employee do exactly as he is instructed, this test is used to make sure that each applicant can and will listen carefully and follow through without extra supervision.

The directions in the test are not hard to follow, but you must listen carefully and do exactly what you are told to do.

In order to do this practice section, you must have a friend who will read the directions to you. *Do not read the material in this section yourself; if you do, you will lose the value of this practice.*

DESCRIPTION OF THE TEST

FOLLOWING ORAL DIRECTIONS - SAMPLE QUESTIONS

The directions are to be read at the rate of 80 words per minute. Since not everybody speaks at this speed, your friend should practice reading the 1-minute practice that follows until he can read it in exactly 1 minute whenever he wants to. He will also need a watch with a second hand. Give the 1-Minute Practice box to your friend to use. (Each friend who is helping you will have to use it to practice, so don't throw it away.)

FOR THE PERSON WHO WILL READ THE FOLLOWING ORAL DIRECTIONS TEST TO YOU

The directions should be read at about 80 words per minute. Practice reading aloud the material in the box below until you can do it in exactly 1 minute. This will give you a feel for the way you should read the test material.

1-MINUTE PRACTICE
(This is for practice in reading aloud. It is not the sample test.)

Look at line 20 in your work booklet. There are two circles and two boxes of different sizes with numbers in them. If 7 is less than 3 and if 2 is smaller than 4, write a G in the larger circle. Otherwise write B as in baker in the smaller box. Now on your Code Sheet darken the space for the number-letter combination in the box or circle.

When your friend reads the directions to you, listen carefully and do what he says. If you fall behind and miss a direction, don't get
excited. Let that one go and listen for the next one. Since B and D sound very much alike, he will say "B as in baker" when he means B and "D as in dog" when he means D.

He will tell you some things to do with the 5 sample questions below. Then, when he tells you to darken a box on the Sample Answer Sheet, use the one on this page.

SAMPLE QUESTIONS

SAMPLE QUESTIONS

QUESTION 1. 5_____

QUESTION 2. 1 6 4 3 7

QUESTION 3. D B A E C

QUESTION 4. (8__) (5__) (2__) (9__) (10__)

QUESTION 5. (7__) [6__] (1__) [12__]

[SAMPLE ANSWER SHEET]

DIRECTIONS to be read. (The words in parentheses should *not* be read aloud. They tell you how long you should pause at the various spots. You should time the pauses with a watch with a second hand. The instruction "Pause slightly" means that you should stop long enough to take a breath.) You should not repeat any directions.

QUESTIONS ON THE SAMPLE

You are to follow the instructions that I read to you. I cannot repeat them.

Look at the Sample Questions. Question 1 has a number and a line beside it. On the line write an A.(Pause 2 seconds.) Now on the Sample Answer Sheet, find number 5 (pause 2 seconds) and darken the box for the letter you just wrote on the line. (Pause 5 seconds.)

Look at Question 2. (Pause slightly.) Draw a line under the third number. (Pause 2 seconds.) Now on the Sample Answer Sheet, find the number under which you just drew a line and darken box B as in baker for that number. (Pause 5 seconds.)

66

Look at the letters in Question 3. (Pause slightly.) Draw a line under the third letter in the line. (Pause 2 seconds.) Now on your . answer sheet, find number 9 (pause 2 seconds) and darken the box for the letter under which you drew a line. (Pause 5 seconds.)

Look at the five circles in Question 4. (Pause slightly.) Each circle has a number and a line in it. Write D as in dog on the blank in the last circle. (Pause 2 seconds.) Now on the Sample Answer Sheet, darken the space for the number-letter combination that is in the circle you just wrote in. (Pause 5 seconds.)

Look at Question 5. (Pause slightly.) There are two circles and two boxes of different sizes with numbers in them. (Pause slightly.) If 4 is more than 2 and if 5 is less than 3, write A in the smaller circle. (Pause slightly.) Otherwise write C in the larger box. (Pause 2 seconds.) Now on the Sample Answer Sheet, darken the space for the number-letter combination in the box or circle in which you just wrote. (Pause 5 seconds.)

Now look at the Sample Answer Sheet. (Pause slightly.) You should have darkened spaces 4B, 5A, 9A, 10D, and 12C on the Sample Answer Sheet.

SUGGESTIONS FOR DOING THE TEST OF FOLLOWING ORAL DIRECTIONS

* Listen carefully to the directions.
* Do exactly what the examiner tells you to do.
* Do not try to get ahead of the examiner.
* If you missed an instruction, wait for the next one.
* Make sure that you darken ONLY one box for each number on the answer sheet.

EXAMINATION SECTION
TEST 1

NOTE: In the examinations the examiner will read aloud directions for you to follow. A sample of directions is given below. The directions are not the same as the directions in the test, but they are somewhat alike. You should have a sheet of lined paper and a pencil as well as the Answer Sheet before you begin.

DIRECTIONS:
1. Fold your lined paper into 4 columns. (Pause for examinee to do this.)
2. In the first column, on the first line, write the number 4. (Pause)
3. On the second line in the same column, write the number 15.
4. Next line, write 12. (Pause)
5. Now go to column 2.
6. Write 35 on the first line (Pause), 26 on the next line, (Pause), and 38 on the third line. (Pause)
7. In column 3, write 11 on the first line (Pause), 18 on the next line (Pause) and 6 last.
8. In column 4, write 16 on the first line next to 4, (Pause), 32 next (Pause) and 19 last.
9. The first number in the first column is 4.
10. Write the letter C next to 4, so it reads 4C. (Pause)
11. The first number in the second column is 35.
12. Write the same letter next to it, so it reads 35C. (Pause)
13. Write C next to the other numbers on the first line, so they read 11C (Pause) and 16C. (Pause)
14. Write the letter A next to each number on the second line, so they read 15A, 26A, etc. (Pause)
15. Write the letter B as in Boy next to each number on the third line. (Pause)
16. Now, take the Answer Sheet you cut out.
17. It has numbers from 1 to 40, and letter spaces.
18. You will mark one space for certain numbers.
19. See how D has been marked for number 1.
20. You will make the same kind of black mark where I tell you. (Pause)
21. Mark 2E. That is, make a black mark at space E for number 2. (Pause)
22. Mark 9C. (Pause)
23. Mark 26C. (Pause)
24. Mark B as in Boy for 15, 16, and 20. (Pause)
25. Mark E for 12, 29, 34, and 39- (Pause)
26. Remember you should *NOT* have more than one mark for any number.
27. If I call a *SECOND* letter for a number where you already have a letter, do *NOT* mark the new letter. Instead, mark the letter A for the number below it.
28. Now I call 2D . You should *1301* mark 2D, because you have already marked 2E. Instead, mark A for the next number.
29. The next number to 2 is 3. So, you should mark 3A. (Pause)
30. Remember to mark A for the *NEXT* number to the one I call if I call a number where you already have a mark.
31. Now I call 28C. (Pause)
32. Next, 9B. (Pause)
33. 17C. (Pause)
34. 12D. (Pause)

35. 26E and 29D. (Pause)
36. Now, take the sheet of lined paper on which you wrote letters and, numbers. (Pause)
37. You will mark the space on your answer sheet for each number and letter you wrote. For example, the first is 4C, so you will mark 4C on your answer sheet.
38. Do *NOT* start until I tell you.
39. Remember: if you have a mark *ALREADY MADE* for a number, do *NOT* mark another letter. If there is already a mark for a number, make *NO* new mark at all.
40. Start to mark, now!

KEY (CORRECT ANSWERS)

1.		11.	C	21.		31.	
2.	E	12.	E	22.		32.	A
3.	A	13.	A	23.		33.	
4.	C	14.		24.		34.	E
5.		15.	B	25.		35.	C
6.	B	16.	B	26.	C	36.	
7.		17.	C	27.	A	37.	
8.		18.	A	28.	C	38.	B
9.	C	19.	B	29.	E	39.	E
10.	A	20.	B	30.	A	40.	

NOTE: ANY OTHER MARK COUNTS AS WRONG. YOU LOSE CREDIT FOR EACH WRONG MARK.

TEST 2

DIRECTIONS: In the test that follows the examiner will read directions aloud and you will mark your -answer sheet as directed.

1. "Mark E for 82, 83, 85, (slight pause) 78, and 102. (Pause)
2. "Mark C for 107, 110, and 103. (Pause)
3. "Mark D as in dog for 101, 110, (slight pause) 76, and 85. (Pause)

"For the next set of questions, mark space E and also mark the letter I call, unless E is already marked. If E is already marked for that number, do not make any mark for that number.

4. "Mark B as in boy for 106, 78, (slight pause) 80, and 84 . (Pause)
5. "Mark A for 108, 104, 83, and 109. (Pause)
6. "Mark C for 79, 102, (slight pause) and 77."

2 (#2)

KEY (CORRECT ANSWERS)

76.	D	86.		96.		106.	B, E
77.	C, E	87.		97.		107.	C
78.	E	88.		98.		108.	A, E
79.	C, E	89.		99.		109.	A, E
80.	B, E	90.		100.		110.	C, D
81.		91.		101.	D		
82.	E	92.		102.	E		
83.	E	93.		103.	C		
84.	B, E	94.		104.	A, E		
85.	D, E	95.		105.			

NOTE: ANY OTHER MARK COUNTS AS WRONG. YOU LOSE CREDIT FOR EACH WRONG MARK.

TEST 3

DIRECTIONS:
1. "Mark B as in boy for 29, 12, 17, 38, 8 . (Pause)
2. "Mark D as in dog for 13, 6, 24, 5. (Pause)
3. "Mark A for 40, 27, 1, 15, 9. (Pause)
4. "Mark E for 13, 39, 31, 4, and 10. (Pause)

"For the next set of questions, mark space E and also mark the letter I call, unless E is already marked. If E is already marked for that number, do *NOT* make any mark for that number.

5. "Mark D as in dog for 12, 9, 19, 23, 2. (Pause)
6. "Mark C for 31, 37, 4, 39. (Pause)
7. "Mark B as in boy for 21, 16, 7, 10, and 26."

KEY (CORRECT ANSWERS)

1.	A	11.		21.	B, E	31.	E
2.	D, E	12.	B, D, E	22.		32.	
3.		13.	D, E	23.	D, E	33.	
4.	E	14.		24.	D	34.	
5.	D	15.	A	25.		35.	
6.	D	16.	B, E	26.	B, E	36.	
7.	B, E	17.	B	27.	A	37.	C, E
8.	B	18.		28.		38.	B
9.	A, D, E	19.	D, E	29.	B	39.	E
10.	E	20.		30.		40.	A

NOTE: ANY OTHER MARK COUNTS AS WRONG. YOU LOSE CREDIT FOR EACH WRONG MARK.

TEST 4

DIRECTIONS:
1. "Mark A for 59, 33, 44, 66, and 75- (Pause)
2. "Mark B as in boy for 69, 42, 31, and 72. (Pause)
3. "Mark E for 35, 64, 58, 47, and 61. (Pause)

"For the next set of questions, mark space B and also mark the letter I call, unless B is already marked. If B is already marked for that number, do NOT mark the new letter. Instead, mark the letter B for the number below it.

4. "Mark D as in dog for 32, 41, 70, and 63. (Pause)
5. "Mark C for 44, 48, 37, 74, and 37 (Pause)
6. "Mark E for 72, 67, 60, 42, and 46. (Pause)
7. "Mark A for 34, 56, 67, 38, and 71."

KEY (CORRECT ANSWERS)

31.	B	46.	B, E	61.	E
32.	B, D	47.	E	62.	
33.	A	48.	B, C	63.	B, D
34.	A, B	49.		64.	E
35.	E	50.		65.	
36.		51.		66.	A
37.	B, C	52.		67.	B, E
38.	B	53.		68.	B
39.	B	54.		69.	B
40.		55.		70.	B, D
41.	B, D	56.	A, B	71.	A, B
42.	B	57.		72.	B
43.	B	58.	E	73.	B
44.	A, B, C	59.	A	74.	B, C
45.		60.	B, E	75.	A

NOTE: ANY OTHER MARK COUNTS AS WRONG. YOU LOSE CREDIT FOR EACH WRONG MARK.

TEST 5

DIRECTIONS:
1. "Mark C for 73, 96, 84, and 80. (Pause)
2. "Mark D as in dog for 68, 88, 99, 91, 78, and 67. (Pause)
3. "Mark E for 70, 93, 82, 75, and 92. (Pause)
4. "Mark B as in boy for 87, 69, 77, 98, and 71. (Pause)

"For the next set of questions, mark space C and also mark the letter I call, unless C is already marked. If C is already marked for that number, do *NOT* mark the new letter. Instead mark the letter A for the number below it.

5. "Mark D as in dog for 72, 89, 92, and 84. (Pause)
6. "Mark A for 66, 95, 77, and 73. (Pause)
7. "Mark B as in boy for 75, 83, 88, 90, 96, 100, and 94."

KEY (CORRECT ANSWERS)

66.	A, C	76.		86.		96.	C
67.	D	77.	A, B, C	87.	B	97.	A
68.	D	78.	D	88.	B, C, D	98.	B
69.	B	79.	C, D	89.	C, D	99.	D
70.	E	80.	C	90.	B, C	100.	B, C
71.	B	81.		91.	D		
72.	C, D	82.	C, D, E	92.	E		
73.	C	83.	B, C	93.	E		
74.	A	84.	C	94.	B, C		
75.	B, C, E	85.	A	95.	A, C		

NOTE: ANY OTHER MARK COUNTS AS WRONG. YOU LOSE CREDIT FOR EACH WRONG MARK.

TEST 6

DIRECTIONS:
1. "Mark E for 50, 37, 19, 24, and 11. (Pause)
2. "Mark B as in boy for 16, 22, 40, and 31. (Pause)
3. "Mark D as in dog for 24, 40, 49, 33,' and 17. (Pause)

"For the next set of questions, mark space D as in dog and also mark the letter I call, unless D is already marked. If D is already marked for that number, do *NOT* mark the new letter. Instead mark the letter E for the number above it.

4. "Mark C for 12, 21, 42, and 29. (Pause)
5. "Mark A for 19, 49, 24, 15, 47, and 40. (Pause)
6. "Mark E for 41, 34, 29, and 17."

KEY (CORRECT ANSWERS)

10.	20.	30.	40. B, D
11. E	21. C, D	31. B	41. D, E
12. C, D	22. B	32.	42. C, D
13.	23. E	33. D	43.
14.	24. D, E	34. D, E	44.
15. A, D	25.	35.	45.
16. B, E	26.	36.	46.
17. D	27.	37. E	47. A, D
18.	28. E	38.	48. E
19. A, D, E	29. C, D	39. E	49. D
			50. E

NOTE: ANY OTHER MARK COUNTS AS WRONG. YOU LOSE CREDIT FOR EACH WRONG MARK.

TEST 7

DIRECTIONS:
1. "Mark D as in dog for 79, 51, 69, 42, and 64.(Pause)
2. "Mark A for 44, 62, 51, 59, 50, 42, 76, and 67. (Pause)
3. "Mark C for 64, 73, 80, 49, 55, and 62. (Pause)

"For the next set of questions, mark space A and also the letter I call, unless A is already marked. If A is already marked for that number, do *NOT* mark the new letter. Instead mark the letter E for that number.

4. "Mark E for 74, 68, 41, 77, and 58. (Pause)
5. "Mark B as in boy for 67, 60, 78, 44, and 76. (Pause)
6. "Mark C for 60, 51, 48, 69, 56, 66, and 79."

KEY (CORRECT ANSWERS)

41.	A, E	51.	A, D, E	61.		71.	
42.	A, D	52.		62.	A, C	72.	
43.		53.		63.		73.	C
44.	A, E	54.		64.	C, D	74.	A, E
45.		55.	C	65.		75.	
46.		56.	A, C	66.	A, C	76.	A, E
47.		57.		67.	A, E	77.	A, E
48.	A, C	58.	A, E	68.	A, E	78.	A, B
49.	C	59.	A	69.	A, C, D	79.	A, C, D
50.	A	60.	A, B, E	70.		80.	C

NOTE: ANY OTHER MARK COUNTS AS WRONG. YOU LOSE CREDIT FOR EACH WRONG MARK.

TEST 8

DIRECTIONS:
1. "Mark C for 37, 8, 29, 23, and 46. (Pause)
2. "Mark E for 50, 4 0, 28, 3, and 29. (Pause)
3. "Mark B as in boy for 38, 26, 23, 45, 47, and 35- (Pause)

"For the next set of questions, mark space C and also the letter I call, unless C... is already marked. If C is already marked for that number, do NOT mark the new letter. Instead mark the letter B for the number that is two below it.V-

4. "Mark D as in dog for 48, 14, 8, 23, 33, 18, and 34. (Pause)
5. "Mark A for 42, 2, 16, 43, and 29. (Pause)
6. "Mark E for 4, 41, 48, and 15."

———

KEY (CORRECT ANSWERS)

1.		16.	A, C	31.	B	46.	C
2.	A, C	17.		32.		47.	B
3.	E	18.	C, D	33.	C, D	48.	C, D
4.	C, E	19.		34.	C, D	49.	
5.		20.		35.	B	50.	B, E
6.		21.		36.			
7.		22.		37.	C		
8.	C	23.	B, C	38.	B		
9.		24.		39.			
10.	B	25.	B	40.	E		
11.		26.	B	41.	C, E		
12.		27.		42.	A, C		
13.		28.	E	43.	A, C		
14.	C, D	29.	C, E	44.			
15.	C, E	30.		45.	B		

NOTE: ANY OTHER MARK COUNTS AS WRONG. YOU LOSE CREDIT FOR EACH WRONG MARK.

TEST 9

DIRECTIONS:
1. "Mark A for 87, 56, 95, 98, 99, 54, 63, and 59. (Pause)
2. "Mark D as in dog for 84, 100, 57, 68, 87, and 60. (Pause)
3. "Mark C for 70, 52, 69, 96, 78, 84, 58, 53, 68, and 76. (Pause)

"For the next set of questions, mark space A and also mark the letter I call, unless A is already marked. If A is already marked for that number, do *NOT* mark the new letter. Instead mark the letter E for the number that is two above it.

4. "Mark B as in boy for 89, 51, 66, 73, 62, and 98. (Pause)
5. "Mark E for 55, 71, 90, 87, 65, 99, and 66. (Pause)
6. "Mark D as in dog for 75, 91, 80, 54, 89, and 95."

2 (#9)

KEY (CORRECT ANSWERS)

51.	A, B	66.	A, B	81.		96.	C, E
52.	C, E	67.		82.		97.	E
53.	C	68.	C, D	83.		98.	A
54.	A	69.	C	84.	C, D	99.	A
55.	A, E	70.	C	85.	E	100.	D
56.	A	71.	A, E	86.			
57.	D	72.		87.	A, D, E		
58.	C	73.	A, B	88.			
59.	A	74.		89.	A, B		
60.	D	75.	A, D	90.	A, E		
61.		76.	C	91.	A, D		
62.	A, B	77.		92.			
63.	A	78.	C	93.	E		
64.	E	79.		94.			
65.	A, E	80.	A, D	95.	A		

NOTE: ANY OTHER MARK COUNTS AS WRONG. YOU LOSE CREDIT FOR EACH WRONG MARK.

TEST 10

DIRECTIONS:
1. "Mark E for 87, 12, 93, 29, 9, 94, 16, 33, 21, 59, 67, 43, and 17. (Pause)
2. "Mark C for 82, 7, 63, 37, 97, 55, 39, 5, 47, and 25 (Pause)
3. "Mark B as in boy for 89, 66, 77, 35, 92, 18, 54, 13, 71, and 30. (Pause)

"For the next set of questions, mark space E and also mark the letter I call unless E is already marked. If E is already marked for that number, do *NOT* mark the new letter. Instead mark the letter D for the number that is three above it and the letter A for the number that is three below it.

4. "Mark A for 91, 62, 14, 87, and 33. (Pause)
5. "Mark B as in boy for 51, 11, 98, 51, 68, and 9. (Pause)
6. Mark C for 56, 4l, 28, 94, 43, and 29."

KEY (CORRECT ANSWERS)

1.	26. D	51. D, E	76.
2.	27.	52.	77. B
3.	28. C, E	53.	78.
4.	29. E	54. A, B	79.
5. C	30. B, D	55. C	80.
6. D	31.	56. C, E	81.
7. C	32. A	57.	82. C
8.	33. E	58.	83.
9. E	34.	59. E	84. D
10.	35. B	60.	85.
11. D, E	36. A	61.	86.
12. A, E	37. C	62. A, E	87. E
13. B	38.	63. C	88.
14. A, E	39. C	64.	89. B
15.	40. D	65.	90. A
16. E	41. C, E	66. B	91. A, D, E
17. E	42.	67. E	92. B
18. B	43. E	68. D, E	93. E
19.	44.	69.	94. E
20.	45.	70.	95.
21. E	46. A	71. B	96.
22.	47. C	72.	97. A, C
23.	48. D	73.	98. D, E
24.	49.	74.	99.
25. C	50.	75.	100.

NOTE: ANY OTHER MARK COUNTS AS WRONG. YOU LOSE CREDIT FOR EACH WRONG MARK.

WORD MEANING
COMMENTARY

DESCRIPTION OF THE TEST
On many examinations, you will have questions about the meaning of words, or vocabulary.

In this type of question you have to state what a word or phrase means. (A phrase is a group of words.) This word or phrase is in CAPITAL letters in a sentence. You are also given for each question five other words or groups of words — lettered A, B, C, D, and E — as possible answers. One of thes words or groups of words means the same as the word or group of words in CAPITAL letters. Only one is right. You are to pick out the one that is right and select the letter of your answer.

HINTS FOR ANSWERING WORD-MEANING QUESTIONS
Read each question carefully.

Choose the best answer of the five choices even though it is not the word you might use yourself.

Answer first those that you know. Then do the others.

If you know that some of the suggested answers are not right, pay no more attention to them.

Be sure that you have selected an answer for every question, even if you have to guess.

SAMPLE QUESTIONS

DIRECTIONS: For the following questions, select the word or group of words lettered A, B, C, D, or E that means MOST NEARLY the same as the word in capital letters. Indicate the letter of the CORRECT answer for each question.

SAMPLE QUESTIONS 1 AND 2

1. The letter was SHORT. SHORT means *MOST NEARLY*

   A. tall   B. wide   C. brief   D. heavy   E. dark

   EXPLANATION
   SHORT is a word you have used to describe something that is small, or not long, or little, etc. Therefore you would not have to spend much time figuring out the right answer. You would choose C. brief.

2. The young man is VIGOROUS. VIGOROUS means *MOST NEARLY*

   A. serious   B. reliable   C. courageous
   D. strong   E. talented

   EXPLANATION
   VIGOROUS is a word that you have probably used yourself or read somewhere. It carries with it the idea of being active, full of pep, etc. Which one of the five choices comes closest to meaning that? Certainly not A. serious, B. reliable, or E. talented; C. courageous — maybe, D. strong — maybe. But between courageous or strong, you would have to agree that strong is the better choice. Therefore, you would choose D.

WORD MEANING

SAMPLE QUESTIONS

In both the Clerk-Carrier and Mail Handler examinations, you will have questions about the meaning of words, or vocabulary. There is a word-meaning part in the Mail Handler examination and a word-meaning section in the Clerk-Carrier examination. The words used in the test for Mail Handler are easier than the ones for Clerk-Carrier.

In this kind of question you have to say what a word or phrase means. (A phrase is a group of words.) This word or phrase is in *italics* in a sentence. You are also given for each question five other words or groups of words---lettered A, B, C, D, and E----as possible answers. One of these words or groups of words means the same as the word or group of words in italics. Only one is right. You are to pick out the one that is right and darken the box that has the letter of your answer.

Hints for Answering Word-Meaning Questions
- Read each question carefully.
- Choose the best answer of the five choices even though it is not the word you might use yourself
- Answer first those that you know. Then do the others.
- If you know that some of the suggested answers are not right, pay no more attention to them.
- Be sure that you have marked an answer for every question, even if you have to guess.

Now study the sample questions and explanations before going on to the Practice Tests.
Word Meaning-Sample Questions
Now try a few.

The letter was *short*. Short means most nearly
- A. tall
- B. wide
- C. brief
- D. heavy
- E. dark

Short is a word you have used to describe something that is small, or not long, or little, etc. There fore you would not have to spend much time figuring out the right answer. You would choose c) brief

Try another.

The young man is *vigorous*. Vigorous means most nearly
- A. serious
- B. reliable
- C. courageous
- D. strong
- E. talented

Vigorous is a word that you have probably used yourself or read somewhere. It carries with it the idea of being active, full of pep, etc. Which one of the five choices comes closest to meaning that? Certainly not A) serious, B) reliable or E) talented; C) courageous-maybe, D) strong-maybe. But between courageous or strong, you would have to agree that strong is the better choice. Therefore you would choose D.

TEST 1

Now that you know what to do, try these. These words are like those in the Mail Handler examination.

For each question, darken the box for the correct answer. Mark your answers on the answer sheet on the next page.

Answer first those questions for which you know the answers. Then work on the other questions. If you can't figure out the answer, guess.

Do not spend more than 30 minutes on this practice test.

1. *Simple* clothing should be worn to work. *Simple* means most nearly

   A. plain
   B. inexpensive
   C. nice
   D. comfortable
   E. old

2. Take your *finished* work to that area of the work floor. *Finished* means most nearly

   A. inspected
   B. assigned
   C. outgoing
   D. completed
   E. rejected

3. If we are not careful, the problem will *develop* further. *Develop* means most nearly

   A. continue
   B. appear
   C. be used
   D. grow
   E. be concerned

4. The mail handler was a *rapid* worker. *Rapid* means most nearly

   A. trained
   B. rash
   C. fast
   D. regular
   E. strong

5. The supply of envelopes is *abundant* for our use. *Abundant* means most nearly

   A. accessible
   B. plentiful
   C. concentrated
   D. divided
   E. scattered

6. The department is working on *experiments* in that area. *Experiments* means most nearly

   A. tests
   B. refinements
   C. statements
   D. plans
   E. patents

7. The members were concerned about two *fundamental* points. *Fundamental* means most nearly

   A. difficult
   B. serious
   C. emphasized
   D. essential
   E. final

8. The leader *asserted* that it was time to start. *Asserted* means most nearly

   A. believed
   B. decided
   C. declared
   D. agreed
   E. contradicted

9. All requests for supplies should be stated *exactly*. *Exactly* means most nearly

   A. briefly
   B. clearly
   C. promptly
   D. emphatically
   E. accurately

10. We had not meant to *alarm* them. *Alarm* means most nearly

    A. endanger
    B. insult
    C. accuse
    D. frighten
    E. confuse

11. The kind of car he bought was *costly*. *Costly* means most nearly

    A. custom made
    B. expensive
    C. desirable
    D. cheap
    E. scarce

12. The cause of the action was *revealed* before the meeting. *Revealed* means most nearly

    A. made known
    B. fully described
    C. carefully hidden
    D. guessed at
    E. seriously questioned

13. The material used to make mail sacks is *durable*. *Durable* means most nearly

    A. thick
    B. waterproof
    C. lasting
    D. elastic
    E. light

14. The *valiant* men and women were rewarded. *Valiant* means most nearly

    A. brave
    B. popular
    C. victorious
    D. loyal
    E. famous

15. The worker was affected by his *fatigue*. *Fatigue* means most nearly

    A. problem
    B. weariness
    C. relaxation
    D. u) sickness
    E. worry

16. The meeting was interrupted by an *urgent* call. *Urgent* means most nearly

    A. trivial
    B. annoying
    C. pressing
    D. surprising
    E. casual

17. The captain of the team will *participate in* the ceremony. *Participate in* means most nearly

    A. depend upon
    B. be recognized at
    C. be invited to
    D. supervise
    E. share in

18. Each office was asked to *restrict* the number of forms it used. *Restrict* means most nearly

    A. watch
    B. record
    C. limit
    D. replace
    E. provide

19. The pole was *rigid*. *Rigid* means most nearly

    A. broken
    B. pointed
    C. bent
    D. rough
    E. stiff

20. The supervisor *demonstrated* the sorting procedure. *Demonstrated* means most nearly

    A. changed
    B. controlled
    C. determined
    D. showed
    E. described

21. The effort was *futile*. *Futile* means most nearly

    A. wasteful
    B. useless
    C. foolish
    D. undesirable
    E. unfortunate

22. There was a pile of *sundry* items on the table. *Sundry* means most nearly

    A. miscellaneous
    B. valuable
    C. unusual
    D. necessary
    E. specific

23. The supervisor should not be *partial*. *Partial* means most nearly

    A. biased
    B. greedy
    C. irresponsible
    D. jealous
    E. suspicious

24. The retired postal worker led an *inactive* life. *Inactive* means most nearly

    A. restful
    B. idle
    C. peaceful
    D. ordinary
    E. weary

4 (#1)

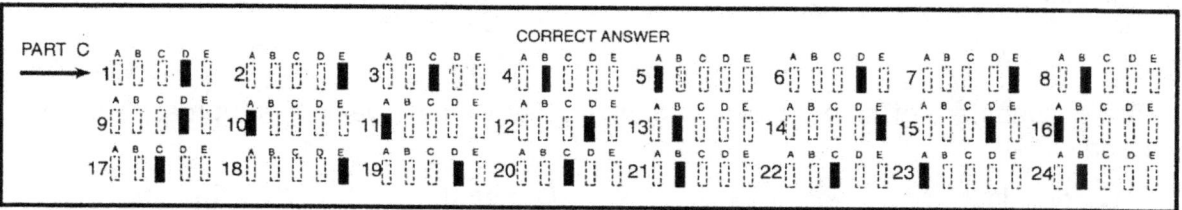

Now check your answers by comparing them with the correct answers shown below.

Count, how many you got right, and write that number on this line _____ _____
(This is your Test Score.)

Meaning of Test Score

If your Test Score is *18 or over,* you have a Good score.

If your Test Score is from *15 to 17,* you have a Fair score.

If your Test Score is *14 or less,* you are not doing too well.

TEST 2

This practice test is a little harder.

For each question, darken the box for the correct answer. Mark your answers on the answer sheet on the next page.

Answer first those questions for which you know the answers. Then work on the other questions. If you can't figure out the answer, guess.

Do not spend more than *30 minutes* on this practice test.

1. The officials *prevented* the action. *Prevented* means most nearly

    A. allowed
    B. urged
    C. hindered
    D. considered
    E. suggested

2. The postmaster's office expected to *report* the results next week. *Report* means most nearly

    A. decide
    B. tell
    C. approve
    D. study
    E. repeat

3. The conference room is now *vacant*. *Vacant* means most nearly

    A. empty
    B. quiet
    C. dark
    D. available
    E. lonely

4. Tapping on the desk can be an *irritating* habit. *Irritating* means most nearly

    A. nervous
    B. annoying
    C. noisy
    D. startling
    E. unsuitable

5. The package was *forwarded* by our office. *Forwarded* means most nearly

    A. returned
    B. canceled
    C. received
    D. detained
    E. sent

6. The postal service is *essential* in this country. *Essential* means most nearly

    A. inevitable
    B. needless
    C. economical
    D. indispensable
    E. established

7. The wheel turned at a *uniform* rate. *Uniform* means most nearly

    A. increasing
    B. unusual
    C. normal
    D. slow
    E. unchanging

8. Each carrier realized his *obligation*. *Obligation* means most nearly

   A. importance
   B. need
   C. duty
   D. n) kindness
   E. honor

9. The group was interested in the *origin* of the rumor. *Origin* means most nearly

   A. direction
   B. growth
   C. existence
   D. beginning
   E. end

10. Laws governing the *parole* of prisoners should be more flexible. *Parole* means most nearly

    A. conditional release
    B. withdrawal of privileges
    C. good behavior
    D. outside employment
    E. solitary confinement

11. That employee is *retiring* by nature. *Retiring* means most nearly

    A. complaining
    B. gruff
    C. neglected
    D. modest
    E. sluggish

12. The patron verified the contents of the package. *Verified* means most nearly

    A. justified
    B. explained
    C. confirmed
    D. guaranteed
    E. examined

13. The group was *repulsed* immediately. *Repulsed* means most nearly

    A. rebuffed
    B. excused
    C. mistreated
    D. loathed
    E. resented

14. The time was right for the committee to make a *decisive* statement. *Decisive* means most nearly

    A. official
    B. prompt
    C. judicial
    D. rational
    E. conclusive

15. Each person expects *compensation* for his work. *Compensation* means most nearly

    A. fulfillment
    B. remuneration
    C. appreciation
    D. approval
    E. recommendation

16. The department plans to increase the number of *novices* in the program. *Novices* means most nearly

    A. volunteers
    B. experts
    C. trainers
    D. beginners
    E. amateurs

17. The guests were overwhelmed by *the fabulous* decorations. *Fabulous* means most nearly

    A. antiquated
    B. enormous
    C. incredible
    D. immoderate
    E. intricate

18. The duties of the job are mentioned *explicitly* in the handbook. *Explicitly* means most nearly

    A. casually
    B. informally
    C. intelligibly
    D. exclusively
    E. specifically

19. The school is supplying opportunities for *recreation*. *Recreation* means most nearly

    A. diversion
    B. eating
    C. resting
    D. learning
    E. recess

20. It was necessary to *recapitulate* the regulation. *Recapitulate* means most nearly

    A. emphasize
    B. withdraw
    C. reinstate
    D. interpret
    E. summarize

21. The villagers *succumbed to* the enemy forces. *Succumbed to* means most nearly

    A. aided
    B. opposed
    C. yielded to
    D. were checked by
    E. discouraged

22. The shipments have been *accelerated*. *Accelerated* means most nearly

    A. anxiously awaited
    B. caused to move faster
    C. delayed by traffic congestion
    D. given careful handling
    E. routed over shorter lines

23. He was not a good employee, because he was *indolent*. *Indolent* means most nearly

    A. stupid
    B. indifferent
    C. selfish
    D. lazy
    E. incompetent

24. He had been cautioned not to be *vindictive*. *Vindictive* means most nearly

    A. boastful
    B. impolite
    C. impulsive
    D. revengeful
    E. aggressive

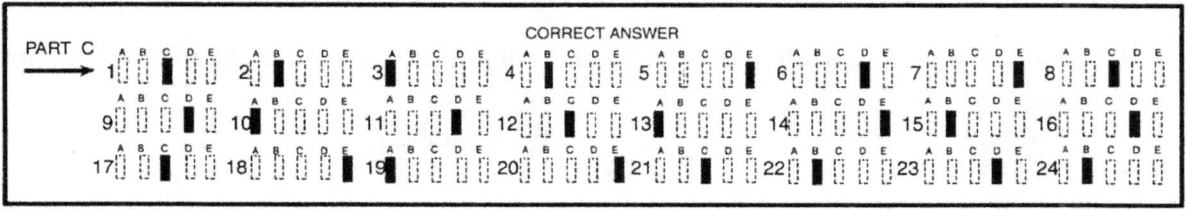

Now check your answers by comparing them with the correct answers shown below.

Count how many you got right, and write that number on this line _____ _____
(This is your Test Score. The meaning of your Test Score will be found on page 3.)

TEST 3

Here is another practice test.

For each question, darken the box for the correct answer. Mark your answers on the answer sheet on the next page.

Answer first those questions for which yon know the answers. Then work on the other questions. If you can't figure out the answer, guess.

Do not spend more than *30 minutes* on this practice test.

1. The *power* of that organization cannot be ignored any longer. *Power* means most nearly

    A. size
    B. courage
    C. success
    D. force
    E. ambition

2. The employees reached the *shore* several days later. *Shore* means most nearly

    A. ocean
    B. reef
    C. island
    D. water
    E. coast

3. The *instructor* was enthusiastic. *Instructor* means most nearly

    A. expert
    B. foreman
    C. teacher
    D. beginner
    E. assistant

4. A *responsible* employee is an asset to any business. *Responsible* means most nearly

    A. considerate
    B. trustworthy
    C. smart
    D. experienced
    E. resourceful

5. He was a good clerk because he was *alert*. *Alert* means most nearly

    A. watchful
    B. busy
    C. honest
    D. helpful
    E. faithful

6. The machine was *revolving* rapidly. *Revolving* means most nearly

    A. working
    B. inclining
    C. vibrating
    D. n) turning
    E. producing

7. The canceling machine did not *function* yesterday. *Function* means most nearly

    A. finish
    B. stop
    C. overheat
    D. vibrate
    E. operate

100

8. The supervisor did not *comprehend* the clerk's excuse. *Comprehend* means most nearly

   A. hear
   B. understand
   C. suspect
   D. consider
   E. accept

9. His conduct was *becoming*. *Becoming* means most nearly

   A. improved
   B. heroic
   C. deliberate
   D. suitable
   E. patient

10. The men were not aware of the *hazard*. *Hazard* means most nearly

    A. peril
    B. choice
    C. decision
    D. contest
    E. damage

11. A *flexible* policy was developed to handle the situation. *Flexible* means most nearly

    A. pliable
    B. weak
    C. rigid
    D. uniform
    E. active

12. The clerk suggested an *innovation*. *Innovation* means most nearly

    A. conventional practice
    B. improvement
    C. inadequate change
    D. new method
    E. preliminary trial

13. Many parents *indulge* their children too much. *Indulge* means most nearly

    A. admire
    B. humor
    C. flatter
    D. coax
    E. discipline

14. The men were *commended* for their actions during the emergency. *Commended* means most nearly

    A. blamed
    B. reprimanded
    C. promoted
    D. encouraged
    E. praised

15. Two men were *designated* by the postmaster. *Designated* means most nearly

    A. dismissed
    B. assisted
    C. instructed
    D. named
    E. rebuked

16. The package will be *conveyed* by the employees. *Conveyed* means most nearly

    A. carried
    B. wrapped
    C. exchanged
    D. refused
    E. guarded

17. It seems *feasible* to start the physical fitness training now. *Feasible* means most nearly

    A. praiseworthy
    B. justifiable
    C. practicable
    D. beneficial
    E. profitable

18. He was a *notorious* rebel. *Notorious* means most nearly

    A. condemned
    B. unpleasant
    C. vexatious
    D. pretentious
    E. well-known

19. The main speaker appeared to be a *pompous* person. *Pompous* means most nearly

    A. narrow-minded
    B. insincere
    C. talkative
    D. self-important
    E. rude

20. The office was surprised that he had *disregarded* his duty. *Disregarded* means most nearly

    A. contemplated
    B. discerned
    C. neglected
    D. resisted
    E. renounced

21. The collector described the *blemish* on the new stamp. *Blemish* means most nearly

    A. color
    B. flaw
    C. design
    D. imprint
    E. figure

22. The *ardor* of the patriot was contagious. *Ardor* means most nearly

    A. anger
    B. desire
    C. zeal
    D. happiness
    E. daring

23. All the employees *vied* for that award. *Vied* means most nearly

    A. contended
    B. cooperated
    C. petitioned
    D. persevered
    E. prepared

24. Immediately after hearing the bad news, the group was in a state of *ferment*. *Ferment* means most nearly

    A. lawlessness
    B. indecision
    C. disintegration
    D. reorganization
    E. agitation

4 (#3)

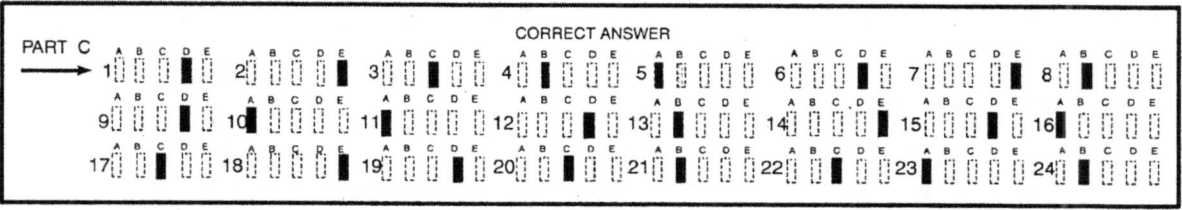

Now check your answers by comparing them with the correct answers shown below.

Count how many you got right, and write that number on this line _____ _____
(This is your Test Score. The meaning of your Test Score will be found on page 3.)

WORD MEANING
EXAMINATION SECTION
TEST 1

DIRECTIONS: For the following questions, select the word or group of words lettered A, B, C, D, or E that means MOST NEARLY the same as the word in capital letters. *PRINT THE LETTER OF THE CORRECT ANSWER IN THE SPACE AT THE RIGHT.*

1. The CONFLAGRATION spread throughout the entire city.

    A. hostilities   B. confusion   C. rumor   D. epidemic   E. fire

2. The firemen PURGED the gas tank after emptying its contents.

    A. sealed   B. punctured   C. exposed   D. cleansed   E. buried

3. Rules must be applied with DISCRETION.

    A. impartiality   B. judgment   C. severity
    D. patience   E. consistency

4. The officer and his men ASCENDED the stairs as rapidly as they could.

    A. went up   B. washed down   C. chopped
    D. shored up   E. inspected

5. The store's refusal to accept delivery of the merchandise was a violation of the EXPRESS provisions of the contract.

    A. clear
    B. implied
    C. penalty
    D. disputed
    E. complicated

6. Mr. Walsh could not attend the luncheon because he had a PRIOR appointment.

    A. conflicting   B. official   C. previous
    D. important   E. subsequent

7. The time allowed to complete the task was not ADEQUATE.

    A. long   B. enough   C. excessive   D. required   E. stated

8. The investigation unit began an EXTENSIVE search for the information.

    A. complicated   B. superficial   C. thorough
    D. leisurely   E. cursory

9. The secretary answered the telephone in a COURTEOUS manner.

    A. businesslike   B. friendly
    C. formal   D. gruff
    E. polite

10. The RECIPIENT of the money checked the total amount.

    A. receiver   B. carrier   C. borrower   D. giver   E. sender

11. The College offered a variety of SEMINARS to upperclassmen.

    A. reading courses with no formal supervision
    B. study courses for small groups of students engaged in research under a teacher
    C. guidance conferences with grade advisors
    D. work experience in different occupational fields
    E. luncheon discussions

12. The Dean pointed out that the FOCUS of the study was not clear.

    A. end   B. objective   C. follow-up   D. location   E. basis

13. The faculty of the Anthropology Department agreed that the departmental program was DEFICIENT.

    A. excellent   B. inadequate   C. demanding   D. sufficient   E. dilatory

14. The secretary was asked to type a rough draft of a course SYLLABUS.

    A. directory of departments and services   B. examination schedule
    C. outline of a course of study   D. rules and regulations
    E. schedule of meetings

15. There is an item in a painting contract relating to INSOLVENCY.

    A. the improper mixing of paint
    B. the use of improper materials
    C. taking excessive time to complete the contract
    D. bankruptcy
    E. the use of water

KEY (CORRECT ANSWERS)

1. E	6. C	11. B
2. D	7. B	12. B
3. B	8. C	13. B
4. A	9. E	14. C
5. A	10. A	15. D

TEST 2

DIRECTIONS: For the following questions, select the word or group of words lettered A, B, C, D, or E that means MOST NEARLY the same as the word in capital letters. *PRINT THE LETTER OF THE CORRECT ANSWER IN THE SPACE AT THE RIGHT.*

1. The number of applicants exceeded the ANTICIPATED figure.   1.____

   A. expected   B. required   C. revised   D. necessary   E. hoped-for

2. The clerk was told to COLLATE the pages of the report.   2.____

   A. destroy   B. edit   C. correct   D. assemble   E. fasten

3. Mr. Jones is not AUTHORIZED to release the information.   3.____

   A. inclined   B. pleased   C. permitted   D. trained   E. expected

4. The secretary chose an APPROPRIATE office for the meeting.   4.____

   A. empty
   B. decorated
   C. nearby
   D. suitable
   E. inexpensive

5. The employee performs a COMPLEX set of tasks each day.   5.____

   A. difficult   B. important   C. pleasant   D. large   E. secret

6. The foreman INVESTIGATED the sewer to see whether it was clogged.   6.____

   A. compelled   B. diverted   C. opened   D. improved   E. examined

7. The foreman SUPERVISED the work closely.   7.____

   A. criticized
   B. neglected
   C. praised
   D. superintended
   E. reviewed

8. ILLICIT connections are often found during sewer inspections.   8.____

   A. damaged   B. legal   C. poor   D. unlawful   E. clogged

9. The sewage in the manhole was floating SLUGGISHLY.   9.____

   A. buoyantly   B. odiferously   C. slowly   D. swiftly   E. evenly

10. It is most COMMON to find sewer pipes made of either clay or concrete.   10.____

    A. characteristic
    B. inordinate
    C. prevalent
    D. retiring
    E. vulgar

11. He needed public assistance because he was INCAPACITATED.   11.____

    A. uneducated
    B. unreliable
    C. uncooperative
    D. discharged
    E. disabled

107

12. The caseworker explained to the client that signing the document was COMPULSORY. 12.___

    A. temporary   B. required
    C. different   D. comprehensive
    E. usual

13. The woman's actions did not JEOPARDIZE her eligibility for benefits. 13.___

    A. delay   B. reinforce   C. determine   D. endanger   E. enhance

14. The material is PUTRESCIBLE. 14.___

    A. compacted   B. liable to burn   C. heavy
    D. liable to rot   E. liable to clog

15. Older incinerator plants are handstoked and fed INTERMITTENTLY. 15.___

    A. constantly   B. heavily   C. periodically
    D. with a shovel   E. every few minutes

KEY (CORRECT ANSWERS)

1. A	6. E	11. E
2. D	7. D	12. B
3. C	8. D	13. D
4. D	9. C	14. D
5. A	10. C	15. C

TEST 3

DIRECTIONS: For the following questions, select the word or group of words lettered A, B, C, D, or E that means MOST NEARLY the same as the word in capital letters. *PRINT THE LETTER OF THE CORRECT ANSWER IN THE SPACE AT THE RIGHT.*

1. The foreman made an ABSURD remark.   1._____

   A. misleading B. ridiculous C. unfair D. wicked E. artful

2. The electrician was ADEPT at his job.   2._____

   A. co-operative
   C. diligent
   E. inept
   B. developed
   D. skilled

3. The foreman stated that the condition was GENERAL.   3._____

   A. artificial B. prevalent C. timely D. transient E. likely

4. The asphalt worker engages in a HAZARDOUS job.   4._____

   A. absorbing B. dangerous C. demanding
   D. difficult E. uninteresting

5. The foreman made a TRIVIAL mistake.   5._____

   A. accidental
   C. obvious
   E. unimportant
   B. dangerous
   D. serious

6. No DEVIATION from the specifications will be allowed unless the same has been previously authorized by the engineer.   6._____

   A. violation B. variation C. complete change
   D. authorized change E. inference

7. The contractor shall SAFEGUARD all points, stakes, grade marks, monuments, and bench marks, made or established on or near the line of the work.   7._____

   A. watch closely
   C. prevent damage to
   E. control
   B. guard against theft
   D. replace

8. Bitumen-sand bed shall consist of sand with cut-back asphalt COMBINED in definite proportions by weight.   8._____

   A. together B. mixed C. added D. placed E. undiluted

9. The material was quite DESICCATED.   9._____

   A. hard B. dangerous C. soft D. spongy E. dry

10. Malice was PATENT in all of his remarks.   10._____

    A. elevated B. evident C. threatening D. foreign E. implicit

11. A Chaplain shall have the COMPARABLE rank of Inspector.

    A. false   B. superior   C. equal   D. presumed   E. ordinary

12. Pushcarts and DERELICT automobiles shall be delivered to the bureau of incumbrances.

    A. dilapidated   B. abandoned   C. delinquent
    D. contraband   E. unusable

13. When the EXIGENCIES of the service shall so require, a captain may assign a patrolman from the outgoing platoon to house duty.

    A. needs   B. conveniences
    C. changes   D. increases
    E. exits

14. There is a provision for the award of a medal for merit for an act of outstanding bravery, performed in the line of duty, at IMMINENT personal hazard of life.

    A. impending   B. inherent   C. certain   D. great   E. eminent

15. A member of the department shall not communicate with a railroad company for the purpose of EXPEDITING the issue of a transportation pass,

    A. extorting   B. procuring   C. demanding
    D. hastening   E. extending

KEY (CORRECT ANSWERS)

1. B	6. B	11. C
2. D	7. C	12. B
3. B	8. B	13. A
4. B	9. E	14. A
5. E	10. B	15. D

TEST 4

DIRECTIONS: For the following questions, select the word or group of words lettered A, B, C, D, or E that means MOST NEARLY the same as the word in capital letters. *PRINT THE LETTER OF THE CORRECT ANSWER IN THE SPACE AT THE RIGHT.*

1. The EXTANT copies of the document were found in the safe.   1.____

    A. existing   B. original   C. forged   D. duplicate   E. torn

2. The recruit was more COMPLAISANT after the captain spoke to him.   2.____

    A. calm   B. affable   C. irritable   D. confident   E. arrogant

3. The man was captured under highly CREDITABLE circumstances.   3.____

    A. doubtful   B. believable   C. praiseworthy
    D. unexpected   E. unbelievable

4. The new employee appeared DIFFIDENT.   4.____

    A. contrary   B. haughty   C. conceited   D. unsure   E. confident

5. His superior officers were more SAGACIOUS than he.   5.____

    A. upset   B. obtuse   C. absurd   D. verbose   E. shrewd

---

KEY (CORRECT ANSWERS)

1. A
2. B
3. C
4. D
5. E

111

Number Series

DESCRIPTION OF THE TEST AND SAMPLE QUESTIONS

This test measures your ability to think with numbers instead of words.

In each problem, you are given a series of numbers that are changing according to a rulefollowed by five sets of 2 numbers each. Your problem is to figure out a rule that would make one of the five sets the next two numbers in the series.

The problems do not use hard arithmetic. The task is merely to see how the numbers are related to each other. The sample questions will explain several types in detail so that you may become familiar with what you have to do.

Hints for Answering Number Series Questions

- Do the ones that are easiest for you first. Then go back and work on the others. Enough time is allowed for you to do all the questions, providing you don't stay too long on the ones you have trouble answering.
- Sound out the series to yourself. You may hear the rule: 2 4 6 8 10 12 14 ... What are the next two numbers?
- Look at the series carefully. You may see the rule: 9 2 9 4 9 6 9 ... What are the next two numbers?
- If you can't hear it or see it, you may have to figure it out by writing down how the numbers are changing: 6 8 16 18 26 28 36 ... What are the next two numbers?
6^{+2} 8^{+8} 16^{+2} 18^{+8} 26^{+2} 28^{+8} 36 ... What are the next two numbers if this is +2 +8? 36+2=38+8=46 or 38 46. You would mark the letter of the answer that goes with 38 46.
- If none of the answers given fit the rule you have figured out, try again. Try to figure out a rule that makes one of the five answers a correct one.

DON'T SPEND TOO MUCH TIME ON ANY ONE QUESTION. SKIP IT AND COME BACK. A FRESH LOOK SOMETIMES HELPS.

Number Series - Sample Questions

Let's try a few
Mark your answers for these samples on the Sample Answer Sheet on this page.

1. 1 2 3 4 5 6 7 ....A) 1 2   B) 5 6   c) 8 9   D) 4 5   E) 7 8

How are these numbers changing? The numbers in this series are increasing by 1 or the rule is "add 1." If you apply this rule to the series, what would the next two numbers be? 7+1=8+1=9. Therefore, the correct answer is 8 and 9, and you would select c) 8 9 as your answer.

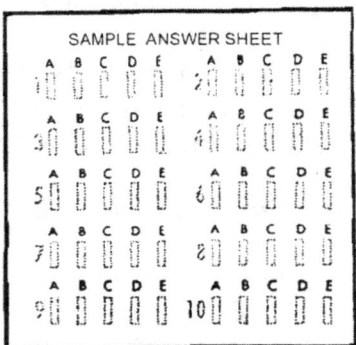

2. 15 14 13 12 11 10 9 .....A) 2 1   B) 17 16   c) 8 9   D) 8 7   E) 9 8

The numbers in this series are decreasing by 1 or the rule is "subtract 1. " If you apply that rule, what would the next two numbers be? 91=81 = 7. The correct answer is 8 and 7, and you would select D) 8 7 as your answer.

3. 20 20 21 21 22 22 23........A) 23 23   B) 23 24   c) 19 19   D) 22 23   E) 21 22

In this series each number is repeated and then increased by 1. The rule is "repeat, add 1, repeat, add 1,
etc." The series would be 20^{+0} 20^{+1} 21^{+0} 21^{+1} 22^{+0} 22^{+1} 23^{+0} 23^{+1} 24. The correct answer is 23 and 24, and you should have darkened B on the Sample Answer Sheet for question 3.

4. 17 3 17 4 17 5 17..........A) 6 17   B) 6 7   c) 17 6   D) 5 6   E) 17 7

If you can't find a single rule for all the numbers in a series, see if there are really two series in the problem. This series is the number 17 separated by numbers increasing by 1, starting with 3. If the series were continued for two more numbers, it would read 17 3 17 4 17 5 17 6 17. The correct answer is 6 and 17, and you should have darkened A on the Sample Answer Sheet for question 4.

5. 1 2 4 5 7 8 10...............A) 11 12   B) 12 14   c) 10 13   D) 12 13   E) 11 13

The rule in this series is not easy to see until you actually set down how the numbers are changing: 1^{+1} 2^{+2} 4^{+1} 5^{+2} 7^{+1} 8^{+2} 10. The numbers in this series are increasing first by 1 (that is plus 1) and then by 2 (that is plus 2). If the series were continued for two more numbers, it would read: 1245 7 8 10 (plus 1) which is 11 (plus 2) which is 13. Therefore the correct answer is 11 and 13, and you should have darkened E on the Sample Answer Sheet for question 5.

Now read and work sample questions 6 through 10 and mark your answers on the Sample Answer Sheet on this page.

6. 21 21 20 20 19 19 18 .... A) 18 18   B) 18 17   C) 17 18   D) 17 17   E) 18 19
7. 1 22 1 23 1 24 1 .... A) 2 61   B) 25 26   C) 25 1   D) 1 26   E) 1 25
8. 1 20 3 19 5 18 7 .... A) 8 9   B) 8 17   C) 17 10   D) 17 9   E) 9 18
9. 4 7 10 13 16 19 22 .... A) 23 26   B) 25 27   C) 25 26   D) 25 28   E) 24 27
10. 30 2 28 4 26 6 24 .... A) 23 9   B) 26 8   C) 8 9   D) 26 22   E) 8 22

The correct answers to sample questions 6 to 10 are: 6B, 7c, 8D, 9D, and 10E.

Explanations for questions 6 through 10.
6. Each number in the series repeats itself and then decreases by 1 or minus 1; *21* (repeat) *21* (minus 1) which makes *20* (repeat) *20* (minus 1) which makes *19* (repeat) *19* (minus 1) which makes *18* (repeat) ? (minus 1) ?
7. The number *1* is separated by numbers which begin with *22* and increase by 1; *1 22 1* (increase 22 by 1) which makes *23 1* (increase 23 by 1) which makes *24 1* (increase 24 by 1) which makes ?
8. This is best explained by two alternating series—one series starts with *1* and increases by 2 or plus 2; the other series starts with *20* and decreases by 1 or minus 1.

    1↑3↑5↑7↑?
    20 19 18 ?

9. This series of numbers increases by 3 (plus 3) beginning with the first number *4* (plus 3) *7* (plus 3) *10* (plus 3) *13* (plus 3) *16* (plus 3) *19*. (plus 3) *22* (plus 3) ? (plus 3) ?
10. Look for two alternating series-one series starts with *30* and decreases by 2 (minus 2); the other series starts with *2* and increases by 2 (plus 2).

    30↑28↑26↑24↑?
    2 4 6 ?

Now try questions 11 to 18. Mark your answers on the Sample Answer Sheet on this page.

11. 5 6 20 7 8 19 9 .... A) 10 18 B) 18 17 C) 10 17 D) 18 19 E) 10 11
12. 9 10 1 11 12 2 13 .... A) 2 14 B) 3 14 C) 14 3 D) 14 15 E) 14 1
13. 4 6 9 11 14 16 19 .... A) 21 24 B) 22 25 C) 20 22 D) 21 23 E) 22 24
14. 8 8 1 10 10 3 12 .... A) 13 13 B) 12 5 C) 12 4 D) 13 5 E) 4 12
15. 14 1 2 15 3 4 16 .... A) 5 16 B) 6 7 C) 5 17 D) 5 6 E) 17 5
16. 10 12 50 15 17 50 20 .... A) 50 21 B) 21 50 C) 50 22 D) 22 50 E) 22 24
17. 1 2 3 50 4 5 6 51 7 8 .... A) 9 10 B) 9 52 C) 51 10 D) 10 52 E) 10 50
18. 20 21 23 24 27 28 32 33 38 39. ...A) 45 46 B) 45 52 C) 44 45 D) 44 49 E) 40 46

HINTS FOR QUESTIONS 11 THROUGH 18.

11. ALTERNATING SERIES: 5 6↑7 8↑9 ?↑
    20 19 ?

12. ALTERNATING SERIES: 9 10↑11 12↑13 ?↑
    1 2 ?

13. INCREASES ALTERNATELY BY 2 (PLUS 2) THEN 3 (PLUS 3) *4* (PLUS 2) *6* (PLUS 3) *9* (PLUS 2) *11* (PLUS 3) *14* (PLUS 2) *16* (PLUS 3) *19* (PLUS 2) ? (PLUS 3) ?

14. ALTERNATING SERIES: 8 8↑10 10↑12 ?↑
    1 3 ?

15. ALTERNATING SERIES: 14↑↑15↑↑16↑ ↑
    12 34 ??

16. ALTERNATING SERIES: 10 12↑15 17↑20 ?↑
    50 50 ?

17. ALTERNATING SERIES: 1 2 3↑4 5 6↑7 8 ?↑
    50 51 ?

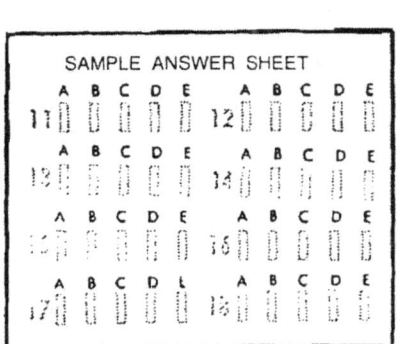

18. INCREASES ALTERNATELY BY (PLUS 1), (PLUS 2), (PLUS 1), (PLUS 3), (PLUS 1), (PLUS 4), ETC. -20 (PLUS 1) 21 (PLUS 2) 23 (PLUS 1) 24 (PLUS 3) 27 (PLUS 1) 28 (PLUS 4) 32 (PLUS 1) 33 (PLUS 5) 38 (PLUS 1) 39 (PLUS 6) ? (PLUS 1) ?

THE CORRECT ANSWERS TO THE SAMPLE QUESTIONS ABOVE ARE: 11A, 12C, 13A, 14B, 15D, 16D, 17B, AND 18A.

NUMBER SERIES-PRACTICE TEST 1

DO FIRST THOSE QUESTIONS THAT YOU CAN DO EASILY. THEN GO BACK AND DO THE ONES THAT YOU SKIPPED.

Work *20 minutes* on this test. No more. No less. If you finish before the 20 minutes are up, go over your answers again. Mark your answers on the Answer Sheet on the next page.

1. 10 11 12 10 11 12 10 .... A) 10 11 B) 12 10 C) 11 10 D) 11 12 E) 10 12
2. 4 6 7 4 6 7 4 .... A) 6 7 B) 4 7 C) 7 6 D) 7 4 E) 6 8
3. 7 7 3 7 7 4 7 .... A) 4 5 B) 4 7 C) 5 7 D) 7 5 E) 7 7
4. 3 4 10 5 6 10 7 .... A) 10 8 B) 9 8 C) 8 14 D) 8 9 E) 8 10
5. 6 6 7 7 8 8 9 .... A) 10 11 B) 10 10 C) 9 10 D) 9 9 E) 10 9
6. 3 8 9 4 9 10 5 .... A) 6 10 B) 10 11 C) 9 10 D) 11 6 E) 10 6
7. 2 4 3 6 4 8 5 .... A) 6 10 B) 10 7 C) 10 6 D) 9 6 E) 6 7
8. 11 5 9 7 7 9 5 .... A) 11 3 B) 7 9 C) 7 11 D) 9 7 E) 3 7

9. 12 10 8 8 6 7 4 .... A) 2 2 B) 6 4 C) 6 2 D) 4 6 E) 2 6
10. 20 22 22 19 21 21 18 .... A) 22 22 B) 19 19 C) 20 20 D) 20 17 E) 19 17
11. 5 7 6 10 7 13 8 .... A) 16 9 B) 16 10 C) 9 15 D) 10 15 E) 15 9
12. 13 10 11 15 12 13 17 .... A) 18 14 B) 18 15 C) 15 16 D) 14 15 E) 15 18
13. 30 27 24 21 18 15 12 .... A) 9 3 B) 9 6 C) 6 3 D) 12 9 E) 8 5
14. 3 7 10 5 8 10 7 .... A) 10 11 B) 10 5 C) 10 9 D) 10 10 E) 9 10
15. 12 4 13 6 14 8 15 .... A) 10 17 B) 17 10 C) 10 12 D) 16 10 B) 10 16
16. 21 8 18 20 7 17 19 .... A) 16 18 B) 18 6 C) 6 16 D) 5 15 E) 6 18

17. 14 16 16 18 20 20 22 .... A) 22 24 B) 26 28 C) 24 26 D) 24 24 E) 24 28
18. 5 6 8 9 12 13 17 .... A) 18 23 B) 13 18 C) 18 22 D) 23 24 E) 18 19
19. 1 3 5 5 2 4 6 6 3 .... A) 7 4 B) 5 5 C) 1 3 D) 5 7 E) 7 7
20. 12 24 15 25 18 26 21 .... A) 27 22 B) 24 22 C) 29 24 D) 27 27 E) 27 24
21. 17 15 21 18 10 16 19 .... A) 20 5 B) 5 11 C) 11 11 D) 11 20 E) 15 14
22. 12 16 10 14 8 12 6 .... A) 10 14 B) 10 8 C) 10 4 D) 4 10 E) 4 2
23. 13 4 5 13 6 7 13 .... A) 13 8 B) 8 13 C) 8 9 D) 8 8 E) 7 8
24. 10 10 9 11 11 10 12 .... A) 13 14 B) 12 11 C) 13 13 D) 12 12 E) 12 13

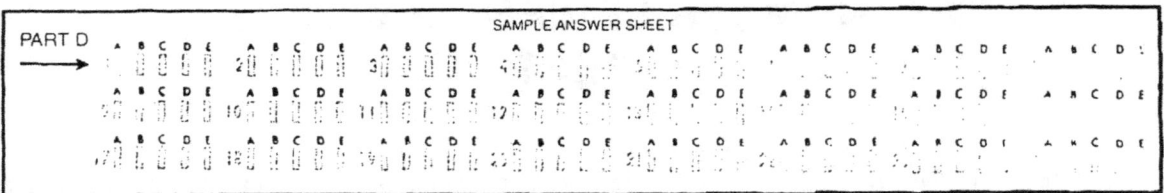

Now check your answers by comparing them with the correct answers shown below.

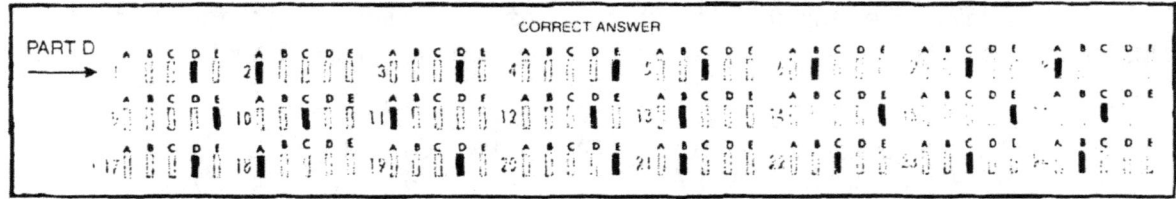

Count how many you got right, and write that number on this line ⟶ _____
(This is your Test Score.)

Meaning of Test Score
  If your Test Score is *17 or more,* you have a Good score.
  If your Test Score *is from 12 to 16,* you have a Fair score.
  If your Test Score is *11 or less,* you are not doing too well.

NUMBER SERIES-PRACTICE
TEST 2

Do first those questions that you can do easily. Then go back and do the ones that you skipped.

Work *20 minutes* on this test. No more. No less. If you finish before the 20 minutes are up, go over your answers again. Mark your answers on the Answer Sheet on the next page.

1. 8 9 9 8 10 10 8 .... A) 11 8   B) 8 13   C) 8 11   D) 11 11   E) 8 8
2. 10 10 11 11 12 12 13 .... A) 15 15   B) 13 13   C) 14 14   D) 13 14   E) 14 15
3. 6 6 10 6 6 12 6 .... A) 6 14   B) 13 6   C) 14 6   D) 6 13   E) 6 6
4. 17 11 5 16 10 4 15 .... A) 13 9   B) 13 11   C) 8 5   D) 9 5   E) 9 3
5. 1 3 2 4 3 5 4 .... A) 6 8   B) 5 6   C) 6 5   D) 3 4   E) 3 5
6. 11 11 10 12 12 11 13 .... A) 12 14   B) 14 12   C) 14 14   D) 13 14   E) 13 12
7. 18 5 6 18 7 8 18 .... A) 9 9   B) 9 10   C) 18 9   D) 8 9   E) 18 7
8. 7 8 9 13 10 11 12 14 13 14... A) 15 16   B) 13 15   C) 14 15   D) 15 15   E) 13 14
9. 5 7 30 9 11 30 13 .... A) 15 16   B) 15 17   C) 14 17   D) 15 30   E) 30 17
10. 5 7 11 13 17 19 23 .... A) 27 29   B) 25 29   C) 25 27   D) 27 31   E) 29 31
11. 9 15 10 17 12 19 15 21 19 .... A) 23 24   B) 25 23   C) 17 23   D) 23 31   E) 21 24
12. 34 37 30 33 26 29 22 .... A) 17 8   B) 18 11   C) 25 28   D) 25 20   B) 25 18
13. 10 16 12 14 14 12 16 .... A) 14 12   B) 10 18   C) 10 14   D) 14 18   E) 14 16
14. 11 12 18 11 13 19 11 14 .... A) 18 11   B) 16 11   C) 20 11   D) 11 21   E) 17 11
15. 20 9 8 19 10 9 18 11 10 .... A) 19 11   B) 17 10   C) 19 12   D) 17 12   E) 19 10
16. 28 27 26 31 30 29 34 .... A) 36 32   B) 32 31   C) 33 32   D) 33 36   E) 35 36

17. 10 16 14 20 18 24 22 .... A) 28 32   B) 27 26   C) 28 26   D) 26 28   E) 27 28
18. 9 9 7 8 7 7 9 10 5 .... A) 5 11   B) 11 12   C) 5 9   D) 9 11   E) 5 5
19. 5 7 11 17 10 12 16 22 15 17 . A) 27 26   B) 19 23   C) 19 27   D) 21 23   E) 21 27
20. 12 19 13 20 14 21 15 .... A) 16 17   B) 22 16   C) 16 22   D) 15 22   E) 15 16
21. 6 6 8 10 10 12 14 .... A) 14 14   B) 14 16   C) 16 16   D) 12 14   E) 10 10
22. 8 1 9 3 10 5 11 .... A) 7 12   B) 6 12   C) 12 6   D) 7 8   E) 6 7
23. 30 11 24 12 19 14 15 17 12 21 10 .... A) 23 8   B) 25 8   C) 26 9   D) 24 9   E) 25 9
24. 24 30 29 22 28 27 19 26 25 15 24 .... A) 14 23   B) 19 18   C) 23 22   D) 25 11   E) 23 10

119

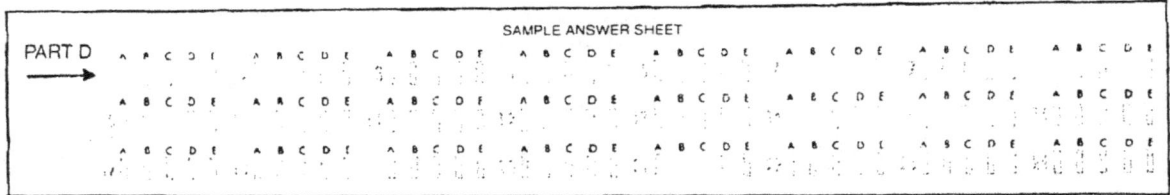

Now check your answers by comparing them with the correct answers shown below.

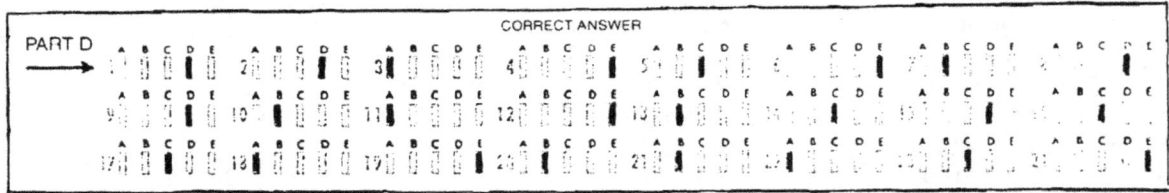

Count how many you got right, and write that number on this line ⟶ _____
(This is your Test Score.)

Meaning of Test Score
    If your Test Score is *17 or more*, you have a Good score.
    If your Test Score *is from 12 to 16*, you have a Fair score.
    If your Test Score is *11 or less*, you are not doing too well.

NUMBER SERIES-PRACTICE
TEST 3

Do first those questions that you can do easily. Then go back and do the ones that you skipped.

Work *20 minutes* on this test. No more. No less. If you finish before the 20 minutes are up, go over your answers again. Mark your answers on the Sample Answer Sheet on the next page.

1. 13 12 8 11 10 8 9 .... A) 8 7   B) 6 8   C) 8 6   D) 8 8   E) 7 8
2. 13 18 13 17 13 16 13 .... A) 15 13 B) 13 14 C) 13 15 D) 14 15 E) 15 14
3. 13 13 10 12 12 10 11 .... A) 10 10 B) 10 9 C) 11 9 D) 9 11 E) 11 10
4. 6 5 4 6 5 4 6 .... A) 4 6   B) 6 4   C) 5 4   D) 5 6   E) 4 5
5. 10 10 9 8 8 7 6 .... A) 5 5   B) 5 4   C) 6 5   D) 6 4   E) 5 3
6. 20 16 18 14 16 12 14 .... A) 16 12 B) 10 12 C) 16 18 D) 12 12 E) 12 10
7. 7 12 8 11 9 10 10 .... A) 11 9   B) 9 8   C) 9 11 D) 10 11 E) 9 10
8. 13 13 12 15 15 14 17 .... A) 17 16 B) 14 17 C) 16 19 D) 19 19 E) 16 16
9. 19 18 12 17 16 13 15 .... A) 16 12 B) 14 14 C) 12 14 D) 14 12 E) 12 16
10. 7 15 12 8 16 13 9 .... A) 17 14 B) 17 10 C) 14 10 D) 14 17 E) 10 14
11. 18 15 6 16 14 6 14 .... A) 12 6 B) 14 13 C) 6 12 D) 13 12 E) 13 6
12. 6 6 5 8 8 7 10 10 .... A) 8 12 B) 9 12 C) 12 12 D) 12 9 E) 9 9
13. 17 20 23 26 29 32 35 .... A) 37 40 B) 41 44 C) 38 41 D) 38 42 E) 36 39
14. 15 5 7 16 9 11 17 .... A) 18 13 B) 15 17 C) 12 19 D) 13 15 E) 12 13
15. 19 17 16 16 13 15 10 .... A) 14 7 B) 12 9 C) 14 9 D) 7 12 E) 10 14
16. 11 1 16 10 6 21 9 .... A) 12 26 B) 26 8 C) 11 26 D) 11 8 E) 8 11
17. 21 21 19 17 17 15 13 .... A) 11 11 B) 13 11 C) 11 9 D) 9 7   E) 13 13
18. 23 22 20 19 16 15 11 .... A) 6 5   B) 10 9 C) 6 1   D) 10 6 E) 10 5
19. 17 10 16 9 14 8 11 .... A) 7 11 B) 7 7   C) 10 4 D) 4 10 E) 7 4
20. 11 9 14 12 17 15 20 18 23 ...... A) 21 24 B) 26 21 C) 21 26 D) 24 27 E) 26 29
21. 7 5 9 7 11 9 13 .... A) 11 14 B) 10 15 C) 11 15 D) 12 14 E) 10 14
22. 9 10 11 7 8 9 5 .... A) 6 7   B) 7 8   C) 5 6   D) 6 4   E) 7 5
23. 8 9 10 10 9 10 11 11 10 11 12 ... A) 11 12 B) 12 10 C) 11 11 D) 12 11 E) 11 13
24. 5 6 8 9 12 13 17 18 23 24 .... A) 30 31 B) 25 31 C) 29 30 D) 25 30 E) 30 37

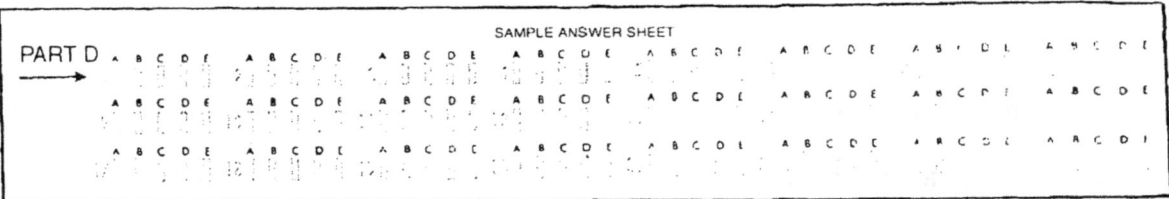

Now check your answers by comparing them with the correct answers shown below.

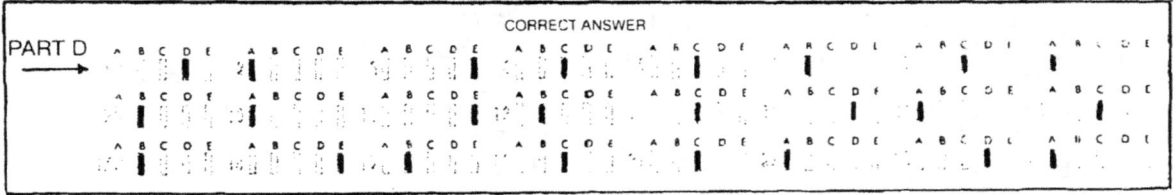

Count how many you got right, and write that number on this line ⟶ _____
(This is your Test Score.)

Meaning of Test Score
    If your Test Score is *17 or more,* you have a Good score.
    If your Test Score *is from 12 to 16,* you have a Fair score.
    If your Test Score is *11 or less,* you are not doing too well.

SAMPLE MAIL HANDLER TEST

Now that you have studied the instructions and taken the practice tests in this book, you are ready to take the Sample Tests. There is one Sample Test for Mail Handler.

The Sample Tests are exactly like the ones you will have to take in the examinations. The time allowances and the numbers of questions are the same as they are in the real tests.

At the back of the book you will find some answer sheets to use. These answer sheets are like the ones you will use in the examinations.

It is a good idea to have a friend tell you when the time is up for each set of sample questions and each part of the test. (There are sample questions for each part.) When you take the Sample Mail Handler Test, you should have a friend read the material in the Following Oral Directions Booklet, which is pages 13 – 15.

After you have finished answering the questions for a sample test, compare your answers with the correct answers for that test and see how well you did.

Mail Handler Test

Time Required for Each Part
- Part A
  - Samples — 3 minutes
  - Test — 6 minutes
- Part B
  - Samples and Test — Approximately 25 minutes
- Part C
  - Samples — 3 minutes
  - Test — 25 minutes

INTERPRETATION OF TEST SCORES ON SAMPLE MAIL HANDLER TEST

After you have taken a Part of the test, or after you have finished the test, compare your answers with those given in the Correct Answers to Sample Test. You will find them on page 12.

For the Address Checking (Part A), count the number that you got right and the number that you got wrong. (If you didn't mark anything for a question, it doesn't get counted.)

From the number right
Subtract the number wrong
This number (the difference) is your score ⟶ _____

The meaning of the score is as follows:

52 or higher	Good.
Between 32 and 51	Fair.
Below 32	You need more practice.

Go back and see where you made your mistakes. Were you careless? Did you work too slowly?

For the Following Oral Directions (Part B), your score is the number right: _____.

The meaning of the score is as follows:

28 or higher	Good.
Between 24 and 27	Fair.
Below 24	You need more practice.

For the Word Meaning (Part C), your score is the number right: _____.

The meaning of the score is as follows:

24 or higher	Good.
Between 20 and 23	Fair.
Below 20	You need more practice.

Go back and see where you made your mistakes. Were you careless? Were there words that you didn't know? If you didn't know the words, try to build up your vocabulary. Some ways of doing this are suggested previously.

SAMPLE MAIL HANDLER TEST

There are three parts to this test. It is best for a friend to time this test for you. (The correct time limits for each part are listed on page 1.) Be sure not to take any more or any less time than given in the instructions for each part.

Tear out an answer sheet from the back of this book and use it to mark your answers for each part.

Directions and Samples for Part A

In this Part you will be given addresses to compare. You are to mark your answer for each question in the row, on your separate answer sheet, that has the same number as the number of the question.

If the two addresses are exactly *Alike* in every way, darken box A. If the two addresses are *Different* in any way, darken box D.

Here are some sample questions for you to do. Mark your answers to them on the Sample Answer Sheet on this page. You should not take more than *3 minutes* to read and study the material on this page of the test.

Keep your mark inside the box on the answer sheet. If you want to change an answer, erase the mark you don't want to count. Then mark your new answer. It will be to your advantage to work as quickly and accurately as possible since your score on this Part will be based on the number of wrong answers as well as the number of right answers. It is not expected that you will be able to finish all the questions in the time allowed.

Be sure to use a No. 2 (medium) pencil.

1 ... Acme La   Acme La

Since the two addresses are exactly alike, you should have darkened box A for question 1 on the Sample Answer Sheet. Now do the other sample questions.

2 ... Orleans Mass   Orleans Mich
3 ... Saxe Va   Saxis Va
4 ... Chappaqua N Y 10514   Chappaqua N Y 10514
5 ... Los Angeles Calif 90013   Los Angeles Calif 90018

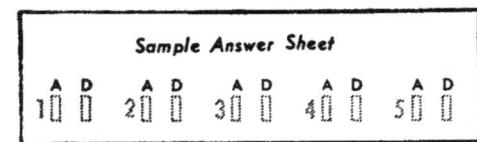

Now compare your answers with the Correct Answers to Sample Questions. If your answers are not the same as the correct answers shown, go back and study the samples to see where you made a mistake.

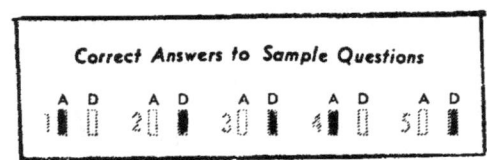

When you begin the test, work as fast as you can without making mistakes. Do as many questions as you can in the time allowed.

Look at your answer sheet. The answers to this part of the examination must be marked in Part A of the answer sheet. Notice also that the answer spaces are numbered across the page. Mark the answer for question 1 in space 1.

You will have *6 minutes* to answer as many of the 95 questions as you can.

DO NOT TURN THIS PAGE UNTIL YOU ARE READY TO BEGIN THE TEST.

PART A

REMEMBER: Mark your answers on the separate answer sheet. Use "A" for "Alike" and "D" for "Different." Work as quickly as you can.

1 ...	Las Vegas Nev	Las Vegas N Mex
2 ...	New Sarpy La	New Sarpy La
3 ...	Loma Mont	Loma Mont
4 ...	Pitsburg Ohio	Pitsburg Ohio
5 ...	Bloomington Ind	Bloomingdale Ind
6 ...	Eastabuchie Miss	Eastabuchie Minn
7 ...	Newberg Oreg	Newberg Oreg
8 ...	Arco Ga	Atco Ga
9 ...	Orocovis P R	Orocovis P R
10 ...	Bloomingburg Ohio	Bloomingdale Ohio
11 ...	Crumpton Md	Crampton Md
12 ...	Nashville Tenn 37214	Nashville Tenn 37214
13 ...	Charlson N Dak	Charlson N Dak
14 ...	Florence S C	Florence S Dak
15 ...	Burnett Minn	Barnett Minn
16 ...	Lakewood Wash	Lakewood Wash
17 ...	Moodus Conn	Moosup Conn
18 ...	Brighton N Y 11200	Brighton N Y 14600
19 ...	Akiak Alaska	Aniak Alaska
20 ...	Maskell Nebr	Maskell Nebr
21 ...	Gaston S C	Gasden S C
22 ...	Sonora Calif 95370	Sonora Calif 95310
23 ...	Glovergap W Va	Clovergap W Va
24 ...	Fairfax Ala	Fairfield Ala
25 ...	Cubero N Mex	Cubero N Mex
26 ...	Reedsville Wis	Reeseville Wis
27 ...	Ada Ohio	Ava Ohio
28 ...	Cheektowaga N Y 14278	Cheektowaga N Y 14278
29 ...	Cayuga N Y	Cayuta N Y
30 ...	Fruitland Idaho	Fruitland Idaho
31 ...	Cora W Va	Cord W Va
32 ...	Afton Tex	Anton Tex
33 ...	Hamptonville N C	Hamptonville N C
34 ...	Portola Calif 96100	Portola Calif 96100
35 ...	Sonoita Ariz	Sonoita Ariz
36 ...	Dunbarton N H 03300	Dunbarton N H 03300
37 ...	Benson Ill	Benton Ill
38 ...	Portland Oreg 97206	Portland Oreg 97206
39 ...	Flayton N Dak	Flaston N Dak
40 ...	Barnsdall Okla	Barnsdall Okla
41 ...	Irmo S C	Irmo S C
42 ...	East Barnet Vt	East Barnet Vt
43 ...	Ellenburg Center N Y 12900	Ellenburg Depot N Y 12900
44 ...	Helena Mo	Helena Mo
45 ...	Grafton Wis	Granton Wis
46 ...	Columbia N C	Columbus N C
47 ...	Dumont Colo	Dupont Colo

GO ON TO NUMBER 48 ON THE NEXT PAGE.

48 ...	McClusky N Dak	McClosky N Dak
49 ...	Sheldon S C	Shelton S C
50 ...	Fredericksburg Iowa	Fredericksburg Iowa
51 ...	Holden Vt	Holton Vt
52 ...	Karlsruhe N Dak	Karlsruhe N Dak
53 ...	East Springfield Pa	West Springfield Pa
54 ...	Villa Prades P R	Villa Prades P R
55 ...	Cadmus Mich	Cadmus Mich
56 ...	New London N H 03200	New London N H 03200
57 ...	Anchorage Alaska 95501	Anchorage Alaska 99501
58 ...	Garciasville Tex 78547	Garciasville Tex 78547
59 ...	Edenton Ohio	Edenton Ohio
60 ...	Vernal Utah	Vernon Utah
61 ...	Tullahassee Okla	Tallahassee Okla
62 ...	Carlton Wash	Carson Wash
63 ...	Tucson Ariz 85721	Tucson Ariz 85751
64 ...	Vermillion S Dak 57069	Vermillion S Dak 57069
65 ...	Oxford N H	Orford N H
66 ...	Evanston Wyo	Evanston Wyo
67 ...	Gonzalez Fla 32560	Gonzalez Fla 32560
68 ...	Clifton Tenn	Clinton Tenn
69 ...	Lindsborg Kans	Lindsborg Kans
70 ...	Greenbush Va	Greenbush Va
71 ...	Paterson N J 07400	Paterson N J 07500
72 ...	Monticello Minn	Monticello Minn
73 ...	Haina Hawaii	Hana Hawaii
74 ...	Barre Mass	Barre Mass
75 ...	Beech Creek Ky 42300	Beech Grove Ky 42300
76 ...	Biddeford Maine 04005	Biddeford Maine 04006
77 ...	Richford N Y	Richland N Y
78 ...	Shamko Oreg 97057	Shaneko Oreg 97057
79 ...	Farmington N Mex	Framington N Mex
80 ...	Goodwell Okla	Goodwell Okla
81 ...	Saginaw Tex	Saginaw Tex
82 ...	Jersey City N J 07323	Jersey City N J 07328
83 ...	Fremont N C	Fremont N C
84 ...	Ottumwa S Dak	Ottumwa S Dak
85 ...	Alasha S Dak	Alaska S Dak
86 ...	Oklahoma City Okla 73106	Oklahoma City Okla 73106
87 ...	Slocum R I	Slocam R I
88 ...	Leesburg Va	Leesburg Va
89 ...	Wilmot Ark	Wilmor Ark
90 ...	Seaford Del 19973	Seaford Del 19973
91 ...	Aldan Pa	Alden Pa
92 ...	Washington D C 20008	Washington D C 20018
93 ...	Wilson Ark	Wilton Ark
94 ...	Fresno Calif 93705	Fresno Calif 93705
95 ...	Clearmont Wyo	Clearmont Wyo

STOP.

If you finish before the time is up, check your answers to this part. Do not go to any other part.

PART B

Part B of the Mail Handler Test is a test of following oral directions. In this Part, have a friend read the directions to you. The instructions, or directions, to be read to you are on pages 13-15. This part of the test will take approximately 25 minutes.

Below are some sample questions as well as a Sample Answer Sheet. Your friend will read the directions to you. Listen carefully.

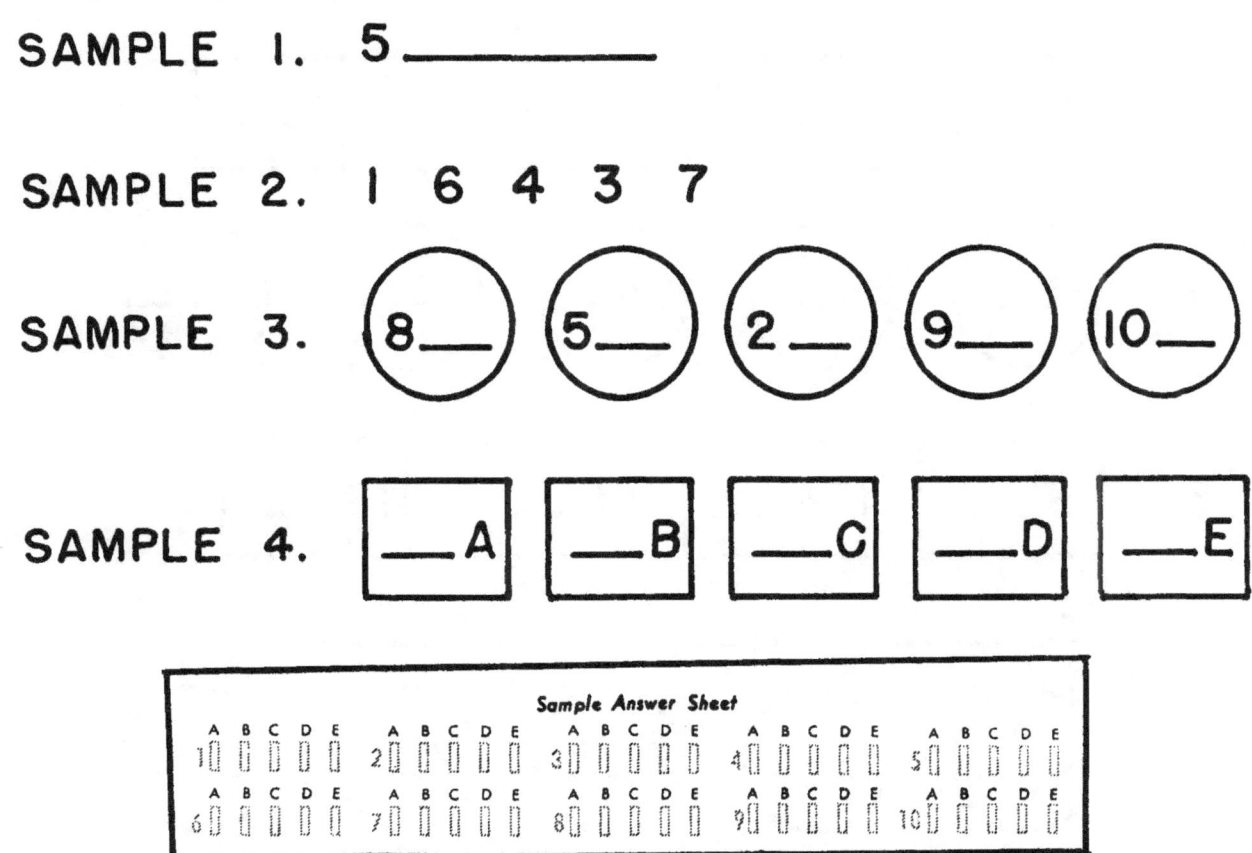

DO NOT GO ON TO THE NEXT PAGE UNTIL YOU ARE TOLD TO DO SO.

1. 13   23   2   19   6

2. E   B   D   E   C   A   B

3. [30__] [18__] [5__] [14__] [7__]

4. (26__) (16__) (23__) (22__) (27__)

5. [3__] [14__] [8__] [18__]

6. 12_____   5_____   22_____

7. (4__) (1__) (6__) (7__) (19__)

8. 26_____   9_____

9. 17   23   11   18   20   32   25   10   9

10. 16   30   13   25   10   14   23   26   19

11. (9:12 __A) (9:28 __B) (9:24 __C) (9:11 __D) (9:32 __E)

12. |17___| |10___| |26___| |8___| |25___|

13. (___A) (___B) (___C) (___D) (___E)

14. |3___| (32___) |20___| (10___)

15. |2___| |31___| |29___| ABLE   EASY   DESK

16. XXOXOOOXOXXOXX

17. (22___) |3___| |21___| (28___)

18. |21___| |8___| |29___| |31___|

19. | 3 DETROIT HARTFORD ___ | | 26 ST. LOUIS CLEVELAND ___ |

___

Sample Questions for Part C

In each question in Part C you are asked what a word or phrase means. In each question a word or phrase is in italics. Five other words or phrases—lettered A, B, C, D, and E—are given as possible meanings of the word or phrase in italics. Only one is *right*. You are to pick out the one that is right. Then on the answer sheet, find the answer space numbered the same as the question, and darken the box under the letter of the right answer.

Here are some sample questions for you to do. Mark your answers to them on the Sample Answer Sheet on this page. Do not spend more than *3 minutes* on reading and studying this page.

1. The letter was *short*. *Short* means most nearly
    A) tall
    B) wide
    C) brief
    D) heavy
    E) dark

In this question the word *short* is in italics. So you are to decide which one of the suggested answers means most nearly the same as *short*. "Brief" means most nearly the same as *short*; so you should have darkened box C for question 1.

2. A crane was used to *raise* the heavy part. *Raise* means most nearly
    A) lift
    B) drag
    C) drop
    D) deliver
    E) guide

Darken the box for your answer. Then compare the answers you have marked with those given in the Correct Answers to Sample Questions.

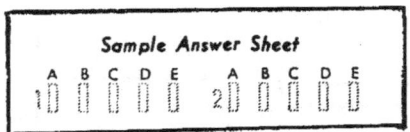

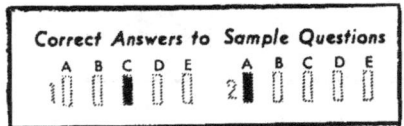

Try to answer every question in this part. Answer first the questions that are easiest for you. Then do the others. If you are not sure of an answer, guess.

You will have *25 minutes* to answer the 32 questions in this part. If you finish before the time is up, go back and check your answers for Part C.

You are to mark your answers to these questions in Part C of your answer sheet.

DO NOT TURN THIS PAGE UNTIL YOU ARE READY TO BEGIN PART C.

PART C

In each question in this part, choose the one of the five suggested answers that means most nearly the same as the word in italics.

Be sure to mark your answers for this part in Part C of the answer sheet.

1. He was asked to *speak* at the meeting. *Speak* means most nearly
   - A) vote
   - B) explain
   - C) talk
   - D) shout
   - E) decide

2. They *discovered* the missing boxes in the morning. *Discovered* means most nearly
   - A) sought
   - B) found
   - C) opened
   - D) noticed
   - E) inspected

3. The number of letters mailed by this office is *double* what it was last year. *Double* means most nearly
   - A) twice
   - B) different from
   - C) more than
   - D) almost
   - E) the same as

4. The post office had to *purchase* the new equipment. *Purchase* means most nearly
   - A) charge
   - B) construct
   - C) supply
   - D) buy
   - E) order

5. The shell was *hollow*. *Hollow* means most nearly
   - A) smooth
   - B) hard
   - C) soft
   - D) rough
   - E) empty

6. The packages were kept in a *secure* place. *Secure* means most nearly
   - A) distant
   - B) safe
   - C) convenient
   - D) secret
   - E) bad

7. It was *customary* for him to be at work on time. *Customary* means most nearly
   - A) curious
   - B) necessary
   - C) difficult
   - D) common
   - E) important

8. An attempt was made to *unite* the groups. *Unite* means most nearly
   - A) improve
   - B) serve
   - C) uphold
   - D) advise
   - E) combine

9. The leader *defended* his followers. *Defended* means most nearly
   - A) praised
   - B) liked
   - C) informed
   - D) protected
   - E) delayed

10. The *aim* of the employees is to do their work well. *Aim* means most nearly
    - A) hope
    - B) purpose
    - C) duty
    - D) promise
    - E) idea

11. The workers will *assemble* the sacks of mail before loading them on the truck. *Assemble* means most nearly
    - A) bring together
    - B) examine carefully
    - C) locate
    - D) fill
    - E) mark

12. The mayor of the city sent a letter to each of the *merchants*. *Merchants* means most nearly
    - A) producers
    - B) advertisers
    - C) bankers
    - D) executives
    - E) storekeepers

13. The clerk was *compelled* to concentrate on his job. *Compelled* means most nearly
    A) tempted
    B) persuaded
    C) forced
    D) unable
    E) content

14. The clerk *extended* his vacation. *Extended* means most nearly
    A) limited
    B) deserved
    C) enjoyed
    D) lengthened
    E) started

15. The *territory* is too large to see in one day. *Territory* means most nearly
    A) swamp
    B) region
    C) city
    D) beach
    E) terminal

16. The technicians *created* a new machine. *Created* means most nearly
    A) planned
    B) copied
    C) invented
    D) tried
    E) replaced

17. The *mended* mail sacks will be delivered. *Mended* means most nearly
    A) repaired
    B) torn
    C) clean
    D) labelled
    E) tied

18. The new post office building is *huge*. *Huge* means most nearly
    A) ugly
    B) tall
    C) sturdy
    D) immense
    E) narrow

19. He was asked to *mingle* with the other guests. *Mingle* means most nearly
    A) consult
    B) visit
    C) sing
    D) mix
    E) dance

20. The director of the program is *likewise* chairman of the committee. *Likewise* means most nearly
    A) also
    B) often
    C) thus
    D) however
    E) meanwhile

21. Doctors are determined to *conquer* the disease. *Conquer* means most nearly
    A) study
    B) fight
    C) overcome
    D) eliminate
    E) trace

22. The machine was *designed* for stamping envelopes. *Designed* means most nearly
    A) fine
    B) used
    C) essential
    D) approved
    E) intended

23. He *mourned* the loss of his friend. *Mourned* means most nearly
    A) resented
    B) grieved
    C) remembered
    D) avenged
    E) faced

24. The meeting will take place at the *usual* time. *Usual* means most nearly
    A) proper
    B) old
    C) customary
    D) best
    E) earliest

25. The employee was given *distinct* instructions. *Distinct* means most nearly
    A) clear
    B) short
    C) new
    D) regular
    E) loud

26. The worker will *bind* the pages together. *Bind* means most nearly
    A) press
    B) receive
    C) make
    D) return
    E) fasten

27. He *startled* the person standing next to him. *Startled* means most nearly
    A) alarmed   D) reassured
    B) touched   E) avoided
    C) scolded

28. He *deceived* them by claiming to be rich. *Deceived* means most nearly
    A) favored   D) imitated
    B) tricked   E) angered
    C) impressed

29. The flood brought *distress* to many families. *Distress* means most nearly
    A) shock   D) risk
    B) illness   E) hunger
    C) suffering

30. Some of the statements made at the meeting were *absurd*. *Absurd* means most nearly
    A) clever   D) foolish
    B) original   E) serious
    C) careless

31. The supervisor *implied* that the schedule would be changed. *Implied* means most nearly
    A) acknowledged D) predicted
    B) imagined   E) insisted
    C) suggested

32. Each person works to earn his own *livelihood*. *Livelihood* means most nearly
    A) salary   D) education
    B) employment   E) maintenance
    C) fortune

If you finish before the time is up, check your answers to this part. Do not go to any other part.

CORRECT ANSWERS FOR MAIL HANDLER TEST

Following Oral Directions Booklet

Important! This booklet is to be read aloud to you; do not read it to yourself.

Instructions to the person who will read the directions

The sample questions are to be read first. All the answers to the samples should be marked on the Sample Answer Sheet.

These instructions should be read at about 80 words per minute. You should practice reading the material in the box until you can do it in exactly 1 minute. This will give you a feel for the way you should read the test material.

> Look at line 20 in your work booklet. There are two circles and two boxes of different sizes with numbers in them. If 7 is less than 3 and if 2 is smaller than 4, write a G in the larger circle. Otherwise write a B as in baker in the smaller box. Now on your code sheet, darken the space for the number-letter combination in the box or circle.

You should read this test aloud before you read it to the person taking the test, in order to acquaint yourself with the procedure and the desired rate of reading.

You should read slowly but at a natural pace. That is, you should not space the words so that there are unnaturally long pauses between them. The instruction "Pause slightly" indicates only enough time to take a breath. The other instructions for pauses give the recommended length of pauses. If possible use a watch with a second hand.

All the material in this booklet except the words in parentheses, starting where indicated below, is to be read aloud.

START READING BELOW:

On the job you will have to listen to directions and then do what you have been told to do. In this test, I will read instructions to you. Try to understand them as I read them; I cannot repeat them. Do not ask questions from now until the end of the test.

You are to write in your booklet according to the directions that I'll read to you. After each set of instructions, I will give you time to mark your answers on an answer sheet.

For each answer you will darken the space for a number-letter combination. When you finish the test, you should have no more than one box marked for each number. If more than one box is marked for a number, it will be counted as an error.

On the job, you won't have to deal with pictures, numbers, and letters like those in the test, but you will have to listen to instructions, and follow them. We are using this test to see how well you can follow instructions.

Before we do the test itself, we will do some samples. Open your book to page 5.

Look at the samples. Sample 1 has a number and a line beside it. On the line write an A. (Pause 2 seconds.) Now on the Sample Answer Sheet on page 5 of your test booklet, find number 7 (pause 2 seconds) and darken the box for the letter you just wrote on the line. (Pause 2 seconds.)

Look at Sample 2. (Pause slightly.) Draw a line under the second number in the line. (Pause 2 seconds.) Now on the Sample Answer Sheet find the number under which you just drew a line and darken box B as in baker for that number. (Pause 5 seconds.)

Now look at the five circles in the third line of samples. (Pause slightly.) Each circle has a number and a line in it. Write a D as in dog on the blank in the last circle. (Pause 2 seconds.) Now on the Sample Answer Sheet darken the space for the number-letter combination that is in the circle you just wrote in. (Pause 5 seconds.)

Now look at the five boxes in Sample 4. Each box has a line and a letter. (Pause slightly.) In the first box write the answer to this question: How many pennies are there in a dime? (Pause 2 seconds.) Now on the Sample Answer Sheet darken the space for the number-letter combination that is in the box you just wrote in. (Pause 5 seconds.)

Now look at the Sample Answer Sheet. (Pause slightly.) You should have darkened spaces 2B, 6D, 7A, and 10A on the Sample Answer Sheet. Did you darken any other space? (Pause slightly.)

You are to mark your test booklet according to the instructions that I'll read to you. After each set of instructions, I'll give you time to record your answers on your regular answer sheet.

In this test, I will read instructions to you. Try to understand them as I read them; I cannot repeat them. Do not ask any questions from now on.

If, when you go to darken a box for a number, you find that you have already darkened another box for that number, either erase the first mark and darken the box for the new combination or let the first mark stay and do not darken a box for the new combination. When you finish, you should have no more than one box darkened for each number.

Turn to the next page in your test booklet.

You will use Part B of your answer sheet for this part of the test.

Look at line 1 in your test booklet. (Pause slightly.) Draw a line under the fourth number in the line. (Pause 2 seconds.) Now, on your answer sheet, find the number under which just drew the line and darken box A for that number. (Pause 5 seconds.)

Look at the letters in line 2 in your test booklet. (Pause slightly.) Draw a line under the fifth letter in the line. Now on your answer sheet find number 15 (pause 2 seconds) and darken the box for the letter under which you drew a line. (Pause 5 seconds.)

Look at the letters in line 2 in your test booklet again. (Pause slightly.) Now draw two lines under the third letter in the line. (Pause 2 seconds.) Now, on your answer sheet, find number 21 (pause 2 seconds) and darken the box for the letter under which you drew two lines. (Pause 5 seconds.)

Look at line 3 in your test booklet. (Pause slightly.) Write an E in the last box. (Pause 2 seconds.) Now, on your answer sheet, find the number in that box and darken box E for that number. (Pause 5 seconds.)

Now look at line 3 again. (Pause slightly.) Write an A in the first box. (Pause 2 seconds.) Now, on your answer sheet, find the number in that box and darken box A for that number. (Pause 5 seconds.)

Look at line 4. The number in each circle is the number of packages in a mail sack. In the circle for the sack holding the largest number of packages, write a B as in baker. (Pause 2 seconds.) Now, on your answer sheet, darken the space for the number-letter combination that is in the circle you just wrote in. (Pause 5 seconds.)

Look at line 4 again. In the circle for the sack holding the smallest number of packages, write an E. (Pause 2 seconds.) Now, on your answer sheet, darken the space for the number-letter combination that is in the circle you just wrote in. (Pause 5 seconds.)

Look at the drawings on line 5 in your test booklet. The four boxes are trucks for carrying mail. (Pause slightly.) The truck with the highest number is to be loaded first. Write a B as in baker on the line beside the highest number. (Pause 2 seconds.) Now, on your answer sheet, darken the space for the number-letter combination that is in the box you just wrote in. (Pause 5 seconds.)

Look at line 6 in your test booklet. (Pause slightly.) Next to the middle number write the letter D as in dog. (Pause 2 seconds.) Now, on your answer sheet, find the space for the number beside which you wrote and darken box D as in dog. (Pause 5 seconds.)

Look at the five circles in line 7 in your test booklet. Write B as in baker on the blank in the second circle. (Pause 2 seconds.) Now, on your answer sheet, darken the space for the number-letter combination that is in the circle you just wrote in. (Pause 5 seconds.)

Now take your test booklet again and write C on the blank in the third circle on line 7. (Pause 2 seconds.) Now, on your answer sheet, darken the space for the number-letter combination that is in the circle you just wrote in. (Pause 5 seconds.)

Now look at line 8 in your test booklet. (Pause slightly.) Write an A on the line next to the right-hand number. (Pause 2 seconds.) Now, on your answer sheet, find the space for the number beside which you wrote and darken box A. (Pause 5 seconds.)

Look at line 9 in your test booklet. (Pause slightly.) Draw a line under every number that is more than 20 but less than 30. (Pause 12 seconds.) Now, on your answer sheet, for each number that you drew a line under, darken box C. (Pause 25 seconds.)

Look at line 10 in your test booklet. (Pause slightly.) Draw a line under every number that is more than 5 and less than 15. (Pause 10 seconds.) Now, on your answer sheet, for each number you drew a line under, darken box D as in dog. (Pause 25 seconds.)

Look at line 11 in your test booklet. (Pause slightly.) In each circle there is a time when the mail must leave. In the circle for the latest time, write on the line the last two figures of the time. (Pause 5 seconds.) Now, on your answer sheet, darken the space for the number-letter combination that is in the circle you just wrote in. (Pause 5 seconds.)

Turn to the next page of the test booklet. (Pause until page has been turned.) Look at the five boxes in line 12 in your test booklet. (Pause slightly.) If 6 is less than 3, put an E in the fourth box. (Pause slightly.) If 6 is not less than 3, put a B as in baker in the first box. (Pause 5 seconds.) Now, on your answer sheet, darken the space for the number-letter combination that is in the box you just wrote in. (Pause 5 seconds.)

Now look at line 13 in your test booklet. (Pause slightly.) There are 5 circles. Each circle has a letter. (Pause slightly.) In the second circle, write the answer to this question: Which of the following numbers is smallest: 32, 11, 22, 31, 16? (Pause 5 seconds.) Now, on your answer sheet, darken the space for the number-letter combination that is in the circle you just wrote in. (Pause 5 seconds.) In the third circle on the same line, write 28. (Pause 2 seconds.) Now, on your answer sheet, darken the space for the number-letter combination that is in the circle you just wrote in. (Pause 5 seconds.) In the fourth circle do nothing. In the fifth circle write the answer to this question: How many months are there in a year? (Pause 2 seconds.) Now, on your answer sheet, darken the space for the number-letter combination that is in the circle you just wrote in. (Pause 5 seconds.)

Look at line 14 in your test booklet. (Pause slightly.) There are two circles and two boxes of different sizes with numbers in them. (Pause slightly.) If 2 is smaller than 4 and if 7 is less than 3, write A in the larger circle. (Pause slightly.) Otherwise write B as in baker in the smaller box. (Pause 2 seconds.) Now, on your answer sheet, darken the space for the number-letter combination in the box or circle in which you just wrote. (Pause 5 seconds.)

Look at the boxes and words in line 15 in your test booklet. (Pause slightly.) Write the second letter of the first word in the third box. (Pause 2 seconds.) Write the first letter of the second word in the first box. (Pause 2 seconds.) Write the first letter of the third word in the second box. (Pause 2 seconds.) Now on your answer sheet, darken the spaces for the number-letter combinations that are in the three boxes you just wrote in. (Pause 10 seconds.)

Look at line 16 in your test booklet. (Pause slightly.) Draw a line under every "O" in the line. (Pause 5 seconds.) Count the number of lines that you have drawn, subtract 2, and write that number at the end of the line. (Pause 5 seconds.) Now, on your answer sheet, find that number and darken space D as in dog for that number. (Pause 5 seconds.)

Look at line 17 in your test booklet. (Pause slightly.) If the number in the left-hand circle is smaller than the number in the right-hand circle, add 2 to the number in the left-hand circle, and change the number in that circle to this number. (Pause 8 seconds.) Then write B as in baker next to the new number. (Pause slightly.) Otherwise write E next to the number in the smaller box. (Pause 3 seconds.) Then, on your answer sheet, darken the space for the number-letter combination that is in the box or circle you just wrote in. (Pause 5 seconds.)

Look at line 18 in your test booklet. (Pause slightly.) If in a year January comes before February, write A in the box with the smallest number. (Pause slightly.) If it does not, write C in the box with the largest number. (Pause 3 seconds.) Now, on your answer sheet, darken the space for the number-letter combination that is in the box you just wrote in. (Pause 5 seconds.)

Now look at line 19 in your test booklet. (Pause slightly.) Mail for Detroit and Hartford is to be put in box 3. (Pause slightly.) Mail for Cleveland and St. Louis is to be put in box 26. (Pause slightly.) Write C in the box in which you put mail for St. Louis. Now, on your answer sheet, darken the space for the number-letter combination that is in the box you just wrote in. (Pause 5 seconds.)

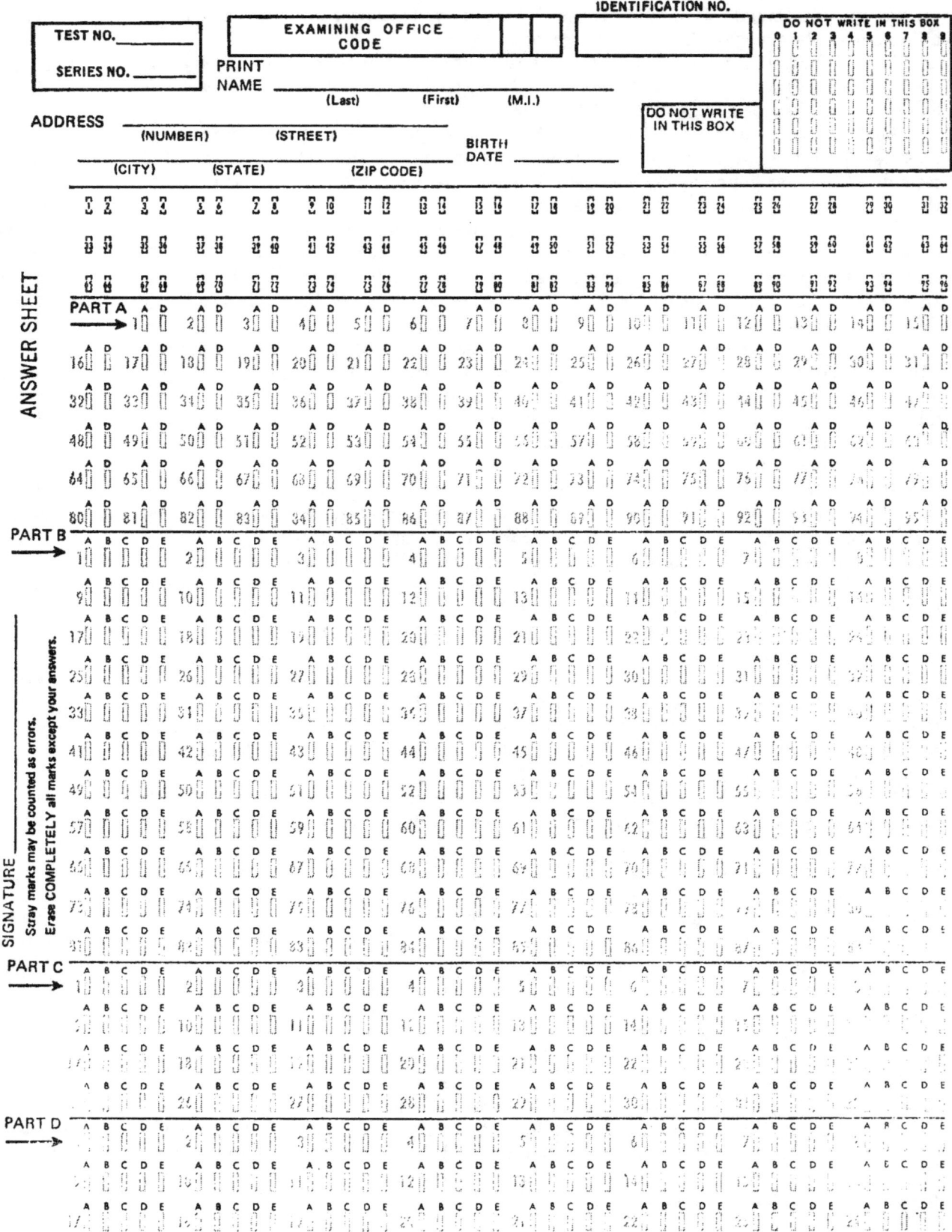

www.ingramcontent.com/pod-product-compliance
Lightning Source LLC
Chambersburg PA
CBHW080736230426
43665CB00020B/2754